Creative
Activities
for the Early Years

Thematic Art and Music Activities

Barbara Melling

Brilliant Publications

With thanks to Amy for her help in the early stages,
Daniel and Matthew for their ideas and inspiration, Rick for his support, April Chapman
for her help with the music and the Reverend Ken Ellis for starting me off.

We hope you and the children you work with enjoy using the ideas in this book. Here are some other early years books published by Brilliant Publications which you might like.

Christmas Activities for the Early Years
Communication, Language and Literacy (Foundation Blocks series)
Creative Development (Foundation Blocks series)
Fun with Action Rhymes and Poems
Fun with Number Rhymes for the Early Years
Games for the Early Years
Knowledge and Understanding of the World (Foundation Blocks series)
Language and Literacy for the Early Years
Mathematical Development (Foundation Blocks series)
Personal, Social and Emotional Development (Foundation Blocks series)
Physical Development (Foundation Blocks series)
Play Activities for the Early Years
Preschool Art
Science and Technology for the Early Years
Springtime Activities for the Early Years
Start with a Song
Storytelling with Puppets, Props and Playful Tales
What Will We Play Today?

Published by Brilliant Publications
1 Church View, Sparrow Hall Farm
Edlesborough
Dunstable
Bedfordshire
LU6 2ES UK

Sales:
Tel: 01202 712910
Fax: 0845 1309300
E-mail: brilliant@bebc.co.uk
Website: www.brilliantpublications.co.uk

The name Brilliant Publications and the logo are registered trademarks.

The publishers apologize if they have inadvertently miscredited anyone for any of the songs and music used in this book. We will correct any mistakes pointed out to us as soon as feasible.

Written by Barbara Melling
Illustrated by Lynda Murray from the original drawings by Barbara Melling
Cover design by Lynda Murray

© Barbara Melling 2006
ISBN 1 903853 710 (978-1-903853-71-9)

First printed and published in the UK in 2006
The right of Barbara Melling to be identified as the author of this work has been asserted by her in accordance with the Copyright, Designs and Patents Act 1988.
10 9 8 7 6 5 4 3 2 1

Contents

Introduction

Having been an art therapist for many years working with both children and adults in many different areas, I have a strong belief that creative self-expression is fundamentally important to our well being. It should be encouraged, enjoyed and valued from babyhood through to old age. I feel that a child is never too young to enjoy making art: as soon as he is able to sit up (on a parent's knee) and hold a crayon, he is ready to experiment and make marks. Equally, even children not yet walking can enjoy music and the bouncing and clapping that go with it. Young children will not need much encouragement to enjoy both making pictures and singing.

Sometimes, however, adults can run out of ideas and that is where this book comes in! *Creative Activities for the Early Years* is for anyone who spends time with babies and young children. Whether you are a leader of a playgroup or nursery, a parent or a carer, I hope you will find this book a useful source of inspiration. There are ideas for something different to do each week of the academic year, including plenty of seasonal themes. You will find easy actions for songs and rhymes and there are simple instructions for home-made instruments, together with suggestions for stories to read and music tapes and CDs to play.

Nurseries and playgroups can use the book methodically and have a different theme every week or, if preferred, they can choose a themed activity whenever they wish by dipping into the book as required.

The book is also aimed at parents and carers at home, who can use it as a useful source of ideas for activities that can be done without a lot of specialist materials and often on a limited budget. Older children will also enjoy many of the activities, making it a handy book for weekends and holidays.

Anyone wishing to start up a creative group for preschool children will be interested in the section entitled 'Setting up a group' (pages 152–156). There is advice on how to put together a weekly group for children and carers, including tips on selecting a suitable venue, local advertising and finding materials, as well as some tried and tested ideas for planning and organising the sessions.

The children will need no encouragement to keep and show off their creative work and it is important that they do so. Valuing a child's work and achievement is one of the most important gifts we, as adults, can give to our children and confidence built at this stage in their life will last forever.

It is worth remembering, finally, that no specialist artistic talent or musical skill is needed to make the most of this book, just plenty of enthusiasm!

How to use this book

The book is set out in weekly sessions to follow the academic year, each session having a different theme. For each session there are at least three art and craft activities, a painting activity, suggested topics to 'talk about', a selection of stories, rhymes, action songs, and suggested musical tapes and CDs for accompanying with instruments or dancing along to. The sessions can be followed from beginning to end for a complete theme, or can be mixed and matched to suit particular needs.

The sessions are divided into three terms, like the school year, starting in September, but can be picked up at any point you choose. Some sessions are best done at certain times of the year – Christmas and Easter for example – but others are interchangable and can be easily moved around to suit a longer or shorter term. It is fun to make the end of term a little special and with this in mind I have included ideas for a party at the end of the Autumn term and for a picnic at the end of the Summer term.

Within each session the activities have been devised to allow all pre-school children a chance to experiment with art materials and create something. This means not only three years and upwards, but also children below this age, who can sometimes be missed out. Each session therefore includes activities with a variety of difficulty.

The art and craft activities have been graded with circles from one to three to allow you to tell at a glance if a little assistance may be needed. Most sessions have a mix of activities. Try to allow the children to decide how they would like to work: by themselves, with a little help occasionally, or as a pair with an adult.

O   Very simple (particularly if some shapes are cut out beforehand)

O O   A little help may be needed for certain tasks

O O O   Some help may be needed. Good for very young children working jointly with an adult

Above all try not to get bogged down, anxious that the finished (or half-finished) work should look like the example. Use that as inspiration, a starting point only, and allow the child to express himself in his own way, without the 'rules' we love to apply. Remember that the sky does not have to be blue and trees do not have to be on the ground – they can just as easily float in the air! Sometimes the children may not know what they have painted, or may not be able to tell you. Accept the work for what it is, a beautiful piece of art. Follow the children's example and let your imagination run away with you!

A wide variety of textures feature in the art and craft activities: wool and materials, rice and grains, hay and straw, dried and fresh leaves, vegetables, twigs, flowers, and many more, as well as the obvious paint and paper. Children love to explore and learn and they can do this through touch and smell as well as sight and sound.

Each activity begins with a 'What you will need' list which gives the main items needed for that art piece. Always have to hand scissors, glue, sticky tape, and a box of bits and pieces such as scrap paper, sweet wrappers and bits of cellophane. Some of the more complicated designs can be found at the back for photocopying, but most of the cut-out shapes that you will need can be done freehand from your imagination or by using the drawings in the book.

Although there are suggestions for many songs and rhymes, the children will have their favourites which they will want to include repeatedly. Children like repetition, so do not be afraid to include the same songs from time to time. Many of the songs appear frequently on CD and tape compilations. For some of the less well-known songs the music has been included. Most of the songs and rhymes are very simple, however, and you can easily make up tunes to fit the words.

Suitable storybooks have also been suggested and, as you will see, some titles are appropriate for more than one theme. Feel free to include a story again if it was popular. As with songs, children love to hear the same stories over and over again.

Craft activities

Underwater collage ⚪

What you will need
* Large sheet of paper (or two or three smaller sheets taped together)
* Wax crayons
* Paper fish shapes (these can be made by the children or in advance)
* Tissue paper
* Dried grains – lentils, rice, etc
* Small shells (optional)

What to do
Colour a large sheet of paper with blue and green wax crayons: hold the crayons sideways and lightly drag them across from side to side. (You can use suitable coloured paper, but colouring your own is a lot better and more fun.)

Glue on fish shapes and strips of torn tissue paper for seaweed. Glue dried grains along the bottom of the picture for the sandy sea bed. Add rocks (paper or scrunched-up tissue), shells, sea creatures, treasure chests – perhaps even a shipwreck!

Try this idea! ✦
Using a very large sheet of paper or lining paper from a roll, make a massive collage together with the whole group. You will have a brilliant result and everyone will enjoy it. If you don't have a wall or table large enough, use the floor!

Fish ●●

What you will need
* Paper (sugar paper or thick paper)
* Photocopiable fish template (page 122)
* Coloured tissue paper
* String

What to do
Cut out a fish shape from the paper (or these can be prepared in advance). Tear off small strips of tissue paper and glue them lengthways along both sides of the fish's body.

Fold the fish in half lengthways (nose to tail) and cut four or five times across the fold, about 1–2cm apart. Be careful not to cut too near to the edge. Leave a good margin of 4–5cm.

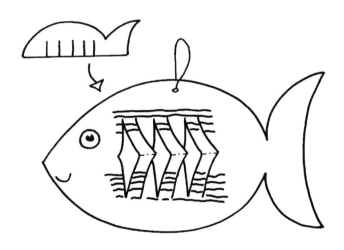

Tip ✦
For best results allow the tissue paper to dry before cutting.

Open the fish and bend the 'cuts' alternately in and out.

Glue an eye onto each side and attach some string to the top of the body so the fish can be hung up.

Jellyfish

What you will need

* Reconstituted paper melon moulds (easily obtained from market stalls and supermarkets)
* Bubble wrap
* String
* Tinsel or strips of shiny paper (optional)

What to do

Cut round the melon moulds to separate them. Do not worry if they are a little uneven. Paint the upturned mould with a bright colour. Cut out and glue on two large eyes and allow to dry. Cut thin strips of bubble wrap at least 30cm long. Glue, tape or staple the strips to the inside of the mould. Attach string for hanging by pushing it through a small hole in the top of the mould and tying a knot on the inside.

Tip
Fold the bubble wrap into a fan shape and cut up the folds. Leave 2cm at the end to attach to the body.

Try this idea!
Add long strips of tinsel or shiny paper inside the top of the mould for an even better jellyfish.

Painting activity

Put out stencils of fish and boats with small rollers or pieces of sponge, saucers of paint, and paper. Even tiny children love stencils, which are easy to obtain from craft shops or pre-school catalogues and last for ever.

Tip
It is a good idea for an adult to steady the stencil until the child is able to do so himself.

Tip
Children will inevitably smudge their pictures or stencil more shapes over their work. Accept this as part of the creative process.

Budget beater
Home-made stencils can easily be made from old cereal boxes – they work just as well but do not last as long.

Talk about

* Has anyone visited the sea?

* Does anyone enjoy swimming - in the sea or swimming pool?

* Fish: How do they swim, breathe?

* Does anyone have a fish?

* Does anyone like fish to eat?

Stories

* *The Snail and the Whale* by Julia Donaldson and Axel Schefflier (Macmillan Children's Books)

* *Fidgety Fish* by Ruth Galloway (Little Tiger Press)

* *Captain Duck* by Jez Alborough (Picture Lions)

Songs and rhymes

One, two, three, four, five

This well-known rhyme can be chanted or sung.

One, two, three, four, five,
Once I caught a fish alive
    count on fingers
Six, seven, eight, nine, ten,
Then I let him go again.
    count on fingers
Why did you let him go?
Because he bit my finger so.
    'bite' little finger with left hand
Which finger did he bite?
This little finger on the right.
    hold up little finger of right hand

Row, row, row the boat

*This well-loved rhyme can be chanted or sung.
(See page 9 for music).*

Row, row, row the boat, gently down the stream
Merrily, merrily, merrily, merrily, life is but a dream.
    *Two people sit facing each other on the floor
    with their legs straight and touching, and
    holding hands. They lean in and out towards
    each other as if rowing.*

Rock, rock, rock the boat, gently to and fro;
Merrily, merrily, merrily, merrily, into the water you go.
    *Rock from side to side and at the end of the
    verse 'fall over' to one side.*

Row, row, row the boat, gently down the stream
If you see a dinosaur (or crocodile), don't forget to
    scream!
    Lean in and out and finally scream loudly.

 **Try this idea!**
Keeping the instruments, try standing and
marching or dancing round the room while
playing to a taped accompaniment.

 Try this idea!
Place a box of instruments on the floor
in the middle of the circle and allow
everyone to help themselves, children
and adults alike. Remain seated and
accompany yourselves to the song.

Bobby Shaftoe

Bobby Shaftoe's gone to sea,
Silver buckles on his knee,
He'll come back and marry me,
Bonny Bobby Shaftoe.

*With the instruments gathered up and everyone
seated you may want to try a calming lullaby. This
is lovely for the children to snuggle up and rock to.*

Good-bye song

*Finish every session with the Good-bye song.
(See page 9 for music).*

Good-bye (Matthew), good-bye (Amy),
Good-bye (Daniel), it's time for us to go.
Good-bye (Hattie), good-bye (Sanjit),
Good-bye (Charley), it's time for us to go.
Good-bye (Lydia), good-bye mummies,
Good-bye everyone, it's time for us to go.

*Just add more lines as necessary so that
everyone is mentioned in the song.*

Other suggestions

❋ Dance to your daddy

❋ Three jellyfish

❋ Rub-a-dub-dub, three men in a tub

❋ A sailor went to sea, sea, sea
    This is fun to sing along to with instruments.

Row, row, row the boat

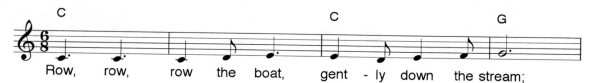

Row, row, row the boat, gent - ly down the stream;

Mer - ril - ly, mer - ril - ly, mer - ril - ly, mer - ril - ly, life is but a dream.

Good-bye song

Good - bye (Matth - ew), good - bye (Amy),

good - bye (Dani - el), it's time for us to go.

Farmyard

Craft activities

Tractor picture

What you will need
* Large sheet of paper
* Photocopiable template of tractor and trailer shapes (page 123)
* Coloured paper
* Hay or dried grass
* Dried grains: rice, split peas, etc (small quantities)

What to do
Cut out a tractor and a trailer shape from coloured paper. Cut out from black paper a large circle for the back wheel, three small circles for the front of the tractor and for the trailer wheels. These can be cut in advance.

Glue all the pieces to a large sheet of paper to form a tractor. Glue a small handful of hay to the top of the trailer (the load).

Draw in the rest of the scene around the tractor – driver, bushes, trees, hills, clouds, etc.

Make another tractor, with grain in the trailer.

> **Tip**
> For the back wheel use a large sticky tape roll as a template.

> **Tip**
> Use lots of glue to stick the hay and grains, otherwise they can drop off!

> **Try this idea!**
> For the road, glue on split peas or rice to look like stones. Scrunched-up green tissue paper makes interesting bushes and trees.

Cows

What you will need
* Thin card
* Photocopiable cow template (page 124)
* Green tissue paper (optional)
* String

What to do
Copy the cow shape onto thin card, fold and cut out. Colour the cow, add eyes and maybe spots. Fray the end of a small piece of string and glue or staple to the inside of the back of the cow for the tail. Glue or staple the cow's head together. Fold under the ends of the feet and glue, staple or tape to a small piece of card. Colour in the ground or glue on scrunched-up green tissue paper for grass.

> **Try this idea!**
> Put everyone's cows together to make a herd.

Creative Activities for the Early Years

Scarecrow ⬤ ⬤ ⬤

What you will need

* A4 piece of thin card
* Scraps of fabric, felt, wool, etc
* Paper

What to do

From the scraps of fabric cut out a jacket and some trousers and glue to the card. Use a small strip of card or paper for the scarecrow's stick. Continue to make up the scarecrow. Use a circle of paper for the head and draw on a face. Glue on a fabric hat and perhaps pieces of yellow wool to the ends of the sleeves and trouser legs for straw. Add some coat buttons, maybe a patch or two on his trousers, and even a crow on his shoulder. Finally draw in the field around the scarecrow.

Tip ☆
Thick fabrics and most felt need a lot of glue to stick properly.

Painting activity

Give the children pieces of plain paper and allow them to paint their own farm scenes, or cut out a basic tractor shape, as big as possible, and let them paint it.

Try this idea!
Cut out some wheels (large and small) in advance and help the children stick them on using the paint as glue.

Note
Town or country, boy or girl – all children love tractors!

Talk about

* How farmers use tractors to help them plant and grow corn in their fields

* How scarecrows are supposed to 'scare the crows' away from the farmer's crops

* How milk comes from cows

Stories

* *Parsnip and the Runaway Tractor* – a lift-the-flap book by Sue Porter (Dorling Kindersley)

* *Tractor in Trouble* and *Scarecrow's Secret* by Heather Amery and Stephen Cartwright (Usborne Publishing)

* *Farmer Duck* by Martin Waddell and Helen Oxenbury (Walker Books)

Songs and rhymes

Baa baa black sheep

This rhyme can be chanted or sung. Make up some simple actions to fit – three fingers held up for three bags full, for example, or join in on the instruments.

Baa baa black sheep,
Have you any wool?
Yes sir, yes sir, three bags full.
One for the master, one for the dame,
And one for the little boy who lives down the lane.

Little boy blue

This rhyme can be chanted or sung. Accompany the rhyme with simple actions such as blowing the horn and pointing to the animals in different directions.

Little boy blue, come blow your horn
There's sheep in the meadow
And cows in the corn!
And where's the boy who looks after the sheep?
He's under the haystack fast asleep.
Will you wake him? No not I,
For if I do he'll be sure to cry.

What does the cow in the field say?

This rhyme is fun to do with or without instruments. Start low and slow and get higher and faster.

What does the cow in the field say?
Mooooooo Mooooooo
What does the dog in the yard say?
Woof Woof Woof Woof
What does the cat on the bed say?
Meeow Meeow Meeow Meeow
What do all the birds in the trees say?
Tweet tweet tweet tweet tweet tweet tweet tweet
tweet tweet tweet tweet TWEET!

Little green frog song

This song is excellent for a good singalong either unaccompanied or together with music. It can be found on many CDs and tapes.

Glub glub went the little green frog one day,
Glub glub went the little green frog.
Glub glub went the little green frog one day,
And the frog went glub, glub, glub,
BUT we know frogs go na na na na na,
Na na na na na, na na na na na,
We know frogs go na na na na na,
They don't go glub, glub, glub.

Quack quack went the little yellow duck one day…

Neigh neigh went the big brown horse one day…

Woof woof went the big shaggy dog one day…

Oink oink went the fat pink pig one day…

Moo moo went the black and white cow one day…

Try this idea!
Keep a collection of small plastic animals featured in the song and hand one to each child for them to hold up high when their verse comes along.

Creative Activities for the Early Years

Old MacDonald

This is a lovely old favourite for singing all together. Sit and sing, or march round the room playing instruments. Many tapes and CDs have this song .

Old MacDonald had a farm
E-I-E-I-O.
And on his farm he had a sheep
E-I-E-I-O.
With a baa baa here, and a baa baa there,
Here a baa, there a baa
Everywhere a baa baa.
Old MacDonald had a farm
E-I-E-I-O

Add further verses with other farmyard animals and machines.

Other suggestions

✱ Scarecrow song
   Children love to do the actions to this popular song which is found on many CDs.

Finish with the Good-bye song on page 8.

Craft activities

Pie picture ⦿

What you will need
* Photocopiable templates for pie dish and pie crust (page 125)
* Paper
* Scraps of coloured tissue, shiny paper, etc

What to do
Before the activity, cut out the pie dish and pie crust shapes. Decorate the pie dish with crayons or pens. Glue the pie dish to a sheet of paper and fill with torn scraps of coloured paper. Make sure the pie crust shape is large enough to cover the filling and attach it to the picture *at the top only* using tape or staples. The crust should lift up to reveal the filling. Add decorations to the crust and steam coming from the top.

Sweet corn collage ⦿

What you will need
* Sheet of paper
* Yellow, orange and gold paper (or small circles already cut out)
* Green paper (or leaves already cut out)

What to do
Draw a stalk on the paper. Cut out small circles from the yellow, orange and gold paper or colour them yourself and glue them onto the stalk on either side. Stick them close together for the best effect. Cut two long leaf shapes from the green paper or colour them yourself and glue them either side of the corn kernels, leaving the yellow circles on show.

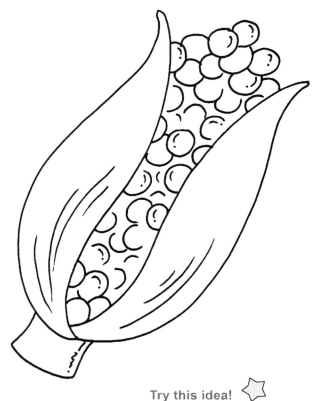

Try this idea! ☆
Bring in a few cobs of sweetcorn (with the leaves on if possible) for all to look at.

Creative Activities for the Early Years

Windmill

What you will need

* Windmills and sails cut from photocopiable template (page 126)
* Sheets of paper
* Straws
* Butterfly clips (paper fasteners)
* Tissue paper, cotton wool

What to do

Glue a windmill shape onto a sheet of paper leaving plenty of room for the sails. Attach a straw lengthways to the back of each of the four sails. Trim the straws to fit. Carefully push a butterfly clip through the thinner ends of each sail (one clip through all four) and attach them to the mill a little way down from the top and in the centre. Open the clip at the back to secure. Add background to the picture: scrunched-up tissue for bushes and trees, clouds, hills and fields.

Tip
Leave the butterfly clip fairly loose so the sails will turn easily when pushed.

Bread

What you will need

* Packets of bread mix (you only need to add water)
* Extra flour
* A selection of seeds, currants and so on to decorate
* Card (cereal boxes are perfect) cut into squares 15 x 15cm
* Tin foil

Tip
Remember to shorten the recommended cooking time to allow for the smaller portions.

Try this idea!
Animals make popular bread shapes, with hedgehogs and mice firm favourites.

What to do

To make a board on which the children can carry home their dough shapes, cover pieces of card with tin foil. Make up the bread mix as directed on the packet and divide into 6–8 portions. Dust a clean surface with a little flour and allow the children to make their own bread shapes. Decorate with currants and such like.

Place the dough shapes on named foil-covered cards ready for taking home or on baking trays to cook on site. If the children are taking their dough home to cook, make sure they know the card trays must not be used for baking.

Painting activity

Allow the children to 'free paint' whatever they wish using paint brushes. Give them as many sheets of paper as possible and not limit them to just one or two.

Talk about

* The time of year and how nature gives us food for the winter

* How grains are ground into flour and how flour can be used for many different foods

* Bread! The many different varieties – white, wholemeal, rolls – what we can do with it (sandwiches, toast, bread and butter pudding)

* Try having some different types of bread for the children to taste!

Stories

* *Good Morning Little Fox* by Marilyn Janovitz (North South Books)

* *Eat Up Pig-little* by Sally Grindley and Andy Ellis (Orchard Books)

* *Little Mouse and the Big Red Apple* by A.H. Benjamin and Gwyneth Williamson (Little Tiger Tales)

Songs and rhymes

Criss cross apple sauce

For this nonsense rhyme the children each sit in front of an adult, who does the actions.

Criss cross
> *draw your finger from left shoulder down to right side and then from right to left*

Apple sauce
> *tap hands on both shoulders*

Spider's walking up your back
> *'walk' fingers up the back*

Cool breeze
> *gently blow on the back of the neck*

Tight squeeze
> *gently hug or squeeze the child*

Now you've got the shivers
> *open arms wide and slowly bring in to tickle child*

Blow wind blow

This little rhyme can be said while the rhythm is tapped out on shakers or drums.

Blow, wind, blow!
And go, mill, go!
That the miller may grind his corn;
That the baker may take it
And into bread make it,
And bring us a loaf in the morn.

Five currant buns

This well-known favourite fits beautifully into this session. (See page 17 for music.)

Five currant buns in the baker's shop,
Round and fat with sugar on the top.
Along came *(child's name)* with a penny one day,
Bought a currant bun and took it away.

Four currant buns… *and so on.*

Try this idea!
Cut five, larger-than-life, simple bun shapes and five big pennies from thin card and decorate. Give one to each children to act out the song as it is sung. Take turns if necessary. The buns and pennies can be used again and again.

© Barbara Melling
www.brilliantpublications.co.uk

Other suggestions

＊ Pat-a-cake, pat-a-cake, baker's man

＊ Food glorious food
Good to sing along to and accompany with instruments.

＊ Teddy bears' picnic
This is lovely for marching to while playing on instruments, or dancing along to. It can be found on many children's CDs and tapes.

Finish with the Good-bye song on page 8.

Five currant buns

Five cur - rant buns in the ba - ker's shop, Round and fat with

sug - ar on the top. A - long came (child's name) with a pen - ny one day,

Bought a cur - rant bun and took it a - way.

Craft activities

Hedgehog

What you will need
* Photocopiable hedgehog template (page 127)
* Thick paper or thin card
* Paper straws (art straws are easily available from pre-school catalogues and are excellent value)
* Sheet of paper (optional)
* Dried leaves (optional)

What to do
Flatten the straws and cut them into short lengths, approximately 3–4cm (these can be prepared in advance), and glue them to the body of the hedgehog. Leave to dry.

Tip
Start at the tail end and work forward overlapping slightly for a more realistic effect.

Paint with brown paint add eyes and feet. Leave to dry. You could glue the hedgehog onto a sheet of paper and glue dried leaves around him for his bed.

Tip
Dried leaves need lots of glue!

Planting bulbs

What you will need
* Small spring-flowering bulbs (1 or 2 per child and a few spare)
* Soil (grow bags are excellent value and last for ages)
* Plastic plant pots measuring about 10cm across (these can be picked up very cheaply from boot fairs or jumble sales) or large yoghurt pots cut down a little
* Sticky labels, or small twigs and paper

Tip
Ask the children about a week in advance to bring in a suitable pot.

What to do
Put the bulbs, pots and soil, together with a light trowel or large spoon, where the children can reach them. Choose somewhere where the soil won't spill and make too much mess. Allow the children to plant their own bulbs.

Decorate the labels and attach one to each pot, or fix a small paper flag to a twig and push into the soil. If the children are unable to write their own name encourage them to draw something on their label or flag.

Tip
Hold this activity away from the others, perhaps on a plastic sheet on the floor in a corner.

Tip
Don't water the bulbs until the pots are safely home.

Creative Activities for the Early Years

Conkers

What you will need

* Photocopiable template for conker and case shapes (page 128)
* Stiff paper
* Butterfly clips (paper fasteners)

What to do

Cut out the conker and case shapes from thick paper. Colour the cut shapes, brown for the conker and green for the case. Draw on a few spikes if you like. Assemble two cases on top of a conker and join at the stalk with a butterfly clip. Spread open the cases to reveal the conker inside.

Try this idea!
Collect a pile of real conkers for the children to handle or suggest they bring some in.

Painting activity

Leaf-printing: place a large pile of leaves (as many different types as possible) on the painting table and allow the children to brush the paint onto the leaves. Press the leaves, paint-side down, onto sheets of paper.

Tip
Use leaves as fresh and as large as possible.

Talk about

* Bulbs: how to plant them with the root pointing down

* How bulbs stay underground through the winter months and grow into flowers in the spring

* Conkers: how they are seeds of the horse chestnut tree; talk about their beautiful colour and how squirrels like to eat them

* How animals such as hedgehogs, hibernate through the winter months and wake up in the spring. Think of other animals that hibernate.

Stories

* *Mr Bear to the Rescue* by Debi Gliori (Orchard Books)

* *Platypus and the Lucky Day* by Chris Riddell (Puffin Books)

* *Bear in Sunshine* by Stella Blackstone (Barefoot Books)

Songs and rhymes

There's a hedgehog in the grass

For the third line, curl up tightly with arms over heads.

There's a hedgehog in the grass –
Do you think he'll let me pass?
Or will he curl up in a ball,
Pretending I'm not here at all!

Brown Bear's snoring

This song can be sung or chanted slowly.

Brown Bear's snoring,
Brown Bear's snoring,
In his winter sleep.
Brown bear's snoring,
Brown bear's snoring,
In his winter sleep.
But snow and ice are melting,
Icicles are dropping,
Brown Bear's ears are listening
And his eyes begin to peep.

Other suggestions

❋ Oranges and lemons

❋ Here we go round the mulberry bush

❋ Underneath the spreading chestnut tree

❋ The wonderful thing about Tiggers
   This song is short, but great fun to 'jig about' to.

Finish with the Good-bye song on page 8.

Flippy floppy hands

This simple action song fits well into any session and may soon become a favourite! Add the actions to the words.

Flippy floppy hands, flippy floppy hands,
Floppy hands, floppy hands,
Flippy floppy hands.

Nodding nodding head…

Shaking shaking shoulders…

Waving waving arms…

Wobbly wobbly legs…

Stretching stretching fingers…

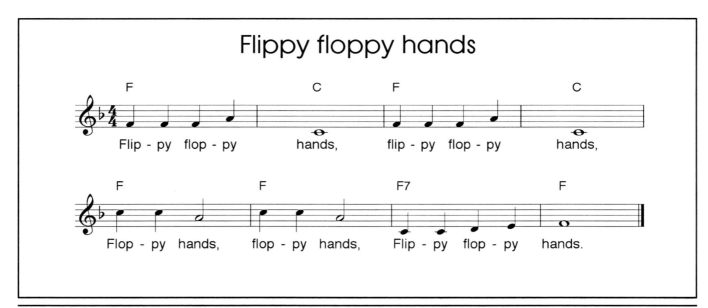

Creative Activities for the Early Years

Craft activities

Chalk drawing

What you will need
* Black paper
* Chalks (large pavement chalks are excellent for small hands)

What to do
Hand out the paper and put out the chalks and allow the children to enjoy themselves! Even the smallest child enjoys making chalk marks.

Try this idea!
Using a roll of black paper, cut as large a piece as you have room for and encourage the children to make lovely big chalk marks, maybe all working together on the floor!

Night-time collage

What you will need
* Sheets of dark blue paper (those which the children have coloured themselves are fun) at least A4 size
* Black skyline shapes (can be pre-cut) to fit the paper
* Full moon shape
* Small star shapes (shop-bought gummed stars can be used)
* Glitter (optional)

What to do
Place the blue paper 'landscape' view. Cut a skyline from black paper, the width of the blue paper and at least 8cm deep and glue onto the bottom of the blue paper. Glue the full moon in the sky. Fill the sky with stars. Cut a few small rectangles from yellow paper and glue them to the black skyline (towards the bottom edge) for lighted windows.

To finish, create some moonlight by lightly dabbing glue onto the rooftops and stars and shaking glitter over the picture. Tip off the excess to be used again!

Try this idea!
Make your skyline as interesting as you can: put in rooftops, a church spire, a block of flats, even a windmill or some trees.

Moon and stars
mobile

What you will need

* ✳ Pea sticks 30cm (these are easily bought from garden shops and cost only pennies)
* ✳ Photocopiable moon and stars template (page 129)
* ✳ Thin card (pre-cut into shapes, if you wish)
* ✳ Thin string or thick cotton
* ✳ Glitter (optional)

What to do

Cut the star, moon and planet shapes from the thin card and decorate them. A little glitter works very well. Thread the thin string or thick cotton through the top of the shapes and attach to a pea stick. Add a loop of string to the middle of the stick so that you can hang the mobile up.

Tip
For more interest vary the length of the strings.

Safety note
Always be careful when using pea sticks with very small children. Do not leave the sticks loose on the table.

For a larger mobile, cross two pea sticks and bind around the middle with sticky tape or string to make an X shape. Attach shapes to both sticks.

Tip
You may need to move the shapes about a little on the stick(s) to achieve the correct balance, so do not tie the strings too tightly.

Try this idea!
Make lots of moons, both full and crescent, and use brightly coloured stars.

Painting activity

Potato printing: cut potatoes into star and moon shapes. Put out saucers of bright paint and allow the children to print onto dark blue and black paper.

Talk about

* ✳ Day turning to night, morning and evening time

* ✳ Bedtime; what do the children do before going to bed?

* ✳ The moon and stars: how the moon changes shape, how the stars appear to twinkle

Stories

* ✳ *Tell Me Something Happy Before I Go To Sleep* by Joyce Dunbar and Debi Gliori (Corgi Childrens)

* ✳ *Peace at Last* by Jill Murphy (Macmillan Children's Books)

* ✳ *Night Night Cuddly Bear* by Martin Waddell and Penny Dale (Walker Books)

Songs and rhymes

These three well-known nursery rhymes can be said, chanted or sung, with or without instruments.

✴ Twinkle, twinkle, little star

✴ Hush-a-bye baby on the treetop

✴ Wee Willie Winkie

Boys and girls come out to play

This well-known rhyme and jolly tune can be found on many tapes and CDs.

Boys and girls come out to play,
The moon does shine as bright as day
Leave your supper and leave your sleep
And join your playfellows out in the street.

Come with a whoop and come with a call
And come with a good will or not at all.
Up the ladder and down the wall
A twopenny loaf will serve us all.
You bring milk and I'll bring flour
And we'll have a pudding in half an hour.

Other suggestions

✴ Bella notte
This lovely gentle song is from Disney's Lady and the Tramp.

✴ Ten in the bed
This jolly song can be sung on it's own or accompanied with instruments.

✴ Morningtown ride
This song is brilliant for calming everyone down or for gentle dancing with scarves.

Finish with the Good-bye song on page 8.

Rabbits

Craft activities

Rabbit's tail

What you will need
* Card (cereal boxes)
* Cotton wool
* Small safety pins

What to do
Cut a card circle approximately 12cm across and glue on cotton wool so that one side is completely covered. Tape a small safety pin onto the back in the middle. (The safety pins could be taped on beforehand.)

Tip ☆
Use a saucer as a template for the tail.

Rabbit's ears

What you will need
* Card (the card from a large cereal box is perfect)
* Cotton wool

What to do
Cut two large rabbit's ears from the card (or these can be cut out in advance) and a strip of card 3–4cm in width and long enough to go round the child's head (two pieces joined together will be fine). Colour the front of the ears pink. Glue cotton wool onto the back and around the edges of the front of the ears. Attach them side by side to the centre of the strip of card using staples or sticky tape.

Fit the card strip around the head of the child and mark the join. Remove and join the ends with sticky tape or staples.

Try this idea! ☆
Use some face paints to draw a twitchy nose and whiskers!

Tip ☆
Always staple outwards so the staple prongs face away from the head.

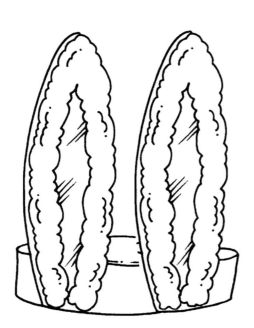

Moving rabbit picture ⬤⬤⬤

What you will need

* ✳ Green A4 paper
* ✳ Stiff paper or thin card
* ✳ Photocopiable rabbit template (page 130)
* ✳ Tissue paper (different greens)
* ✳ Straws
* ✳ Cotton wool (small amount)

What to do

Place the A4 paper 'landscape' view. Cut a rabbit shape from stiff paper. Colour it and glue on a little piece of cotton wool for a tail. Make a small hole, the size of the end of the straw, in the middle of the paper a little below the centre. Attach the rabbit to one end of the straw with sticky tape, push the other end through the hole in the paper so the straw can be pulled from behind. Keep in place with a small piece of paper. Draw a rabbit burrow around the hole in the paper and add a few bushes with scrunched-up tissue paper. Finish the drawing with some hills or a field, a few clouds and birds, and maybe a rainbow.

Turn the paper over. Tape a piece of scrap paper over the straw so that it stays level with the hole while still being able to move to and fro.

Try this idea! ⭐
Bushes made from tissue paper around the top edge of the burrow will help the rabbit disappear.

Painting activity

Carrots! Cut huge carrot shapes from sheets of paper (the bigger the better). Place orange, red and yellow paint together with brushes or sponges on the table. Paint the carrots. Cut long strips of green tissue or crepe paper 2–3cm wide and at least 30cm long. Attach the strips to the top of the carrot with sticky tape. The long leaves will hang down and look lovely.

Try this idea!
The carrots make the perfect accesssory for a child-sized rabbit!

Talk about

* ✳ Pets: children love to talk about their pets

* ✳ Where do rabbits live? Wild rabbits in burrows and pet rabbits in hutches

* ✳ What do rabbits like to eat? Grass, other vegetables…

* ✳ Why do they have such big ears?

Stories

✳ *Whose Ears?* by David Bennett and Julie Lacome (Mammoth)

✳ *The Tale of Peter Rabbit* by Beatrix Potter (Frederick Warne)

✳ *Blue Rabbit and Friends* by Chris Wormell (Red Fox)

Songs and rhymes

Sleeping bunnies

This is an absolute favourite which children will ask for again and again! (See page 27 for music.)

See the little bunnies sleeping till it's nearly noon.
Shall we wake them, gently wake them with this
　　happy tune?
Oh so still. Are they ill?
NO!
Hop little bunnies hop, hop, hop
Hop little bunnies hop, hop, hop,
Hop little bunnies hop, hop, hop,
Hop little bunnies hop, hop, stop!

The children can all lie on the floor and pretend to sleep until the question 'Are they ill?' when they all jump up and shout 'No!' The children then hop about while the adults clap their hands to the tune – or the adults can hop too, if they wish!

Little Peter Rabbit

This song is sung to the tune of 'John Brown's body.'

Little Peter Rabbit had a fly upon his nose,
Little Peter Rabbit had a fly upon his nose,
Little Peter Rabbit had a fly upon his nose,
　　*children kneel on floor with hands held up for
　　bunny ears and wrinkle their noses*
So he flipped it and he flopped it
'Till the fly flew away.
　　*brush fly away with first one hand then the
　　other, 'follow' fly with fluttering fingers as it
　　flies away*
Fluffy tail and curly whiskers,
Fluffy tail and curly whiskers,
Fluffy tail and curly whiskers,
　　*stick out bottom and tap it for fluffy tail and
　　twist fingers outwards from face for curly
　　whiskers*
So he flipped it and he flopped it
'Till the fly flew away.
　　brush fly away and so on

Other suggestions

✳ *Do your ears hang low?*
This jolly song is fun to dance along to with or without instruments or scarves.

Finish with the Good-bye song on page 8.

© Barbara Melling
www.brilliantpublications.co.uk

Sleeping bunnies

See the lit - tle bun - nies slee - ping till it's near - ly noon.

Shall we wake them, gent - ly wake them with this hap - py tune?

Oh so still. Are they ill? NO! Hop lit - tle bun -nies, hop, hop, hop,

Hop lit - tle bun - nies, hop, hop, hop, Hop lit - tle bun - nies,

hop, hop, hop, Hop lit - tle bun - nies, hop, hop, stop!

Halloween

Note
Some people feel strongly that Halloween should not be celebrated, because of its pagan origins. Sound out parents' views prior to this session, and if necessary skip it.

Craft activities

Pumpkin ⬤

What you will need
* Orange paper
* Green paper
* Black paper (bought or coloured)

What to do
Cut a pumpkin shape from orange paper, the larger the better (these can be cut out in advance). Cut a stalk shape from the green paper to fit the top of the pumpkin and eye, nose and mouth shapes from the black paper (these can also be cut out in advance). Tip, use off-cuts left over from the Night-time Skyline. Have lots of different sized triangles for eyes and noses and allow the children to help themselves (but don't be surprised if the pumpkins have seven eyes and four noses). Glue the shapes to the pumpkin to make a face.

> **Try this idea!** ✩
> Make lots of different faces – happy, sad, surprised, scary…

> **Try this idea!** ✩
> Why not have a real pumpkin (with a face cut in it) on the table to show the children?

Fir cone spiders ⬤

What you will need
* Fir cones (you can use any conkers, but don't try to hang them up as they will be too heavy)
* Straws

What to do
Bend four straws in half to find the middle then straighten them out again. These are the eight legs of the spider. Tape them together so they are attached in the centre. Using lots of glue, stick a fir cone over the middle and push it on firmly. This is the spider's body. Add some eyes. Turn the ends of the straws out to make little feet.

> **Try this idea!** ✩
> Why not attach a piece of cotton to the top of the spider and dangle him as a mobile?

Bats

What you will need
* Black paper
* Photocopiable bat template (page 131)
* Thin string
* Glitter (optional)

What to do
Cut a bat shape from the black paper (or use ones you have cut out in advance).

Tip
Fold the paper in half, draw half the bat shape and cut out. This way you get a perfectly symmetrical bat.

Open out the bat and keeping the fold upwards attach the thin string to the top of the bat's back. Fold the ears up and add some eyes. Dab with glue and sprinkle with glitter for an extra special bat. Tie a loop in the end of the string for easier hanging.

Try this idea!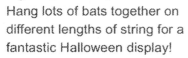
Hang lots of bats together on different lengths of string for a fantastic Halloween display!

Witch or wizard hats

What you will need
* Large sheets of black paper
* Shiny paper
* Tissue paper

What to do
Make the black paper into a cone shape the size of the child's head. Secure with tape and trim around the bottom for an even edge. Tear some strips of coloured tissue paper for hair (green or purple are excellent witch colours) and tape them to the inside of the rim. Decorate the hat with gold and silver stars and moons.

Budget beater
Collect sweet wrappers for a good supply of shiny paper that is perfect for stars and moons.

Painting activity
Potato-printing with simple Halloween shapes such as a witch's hat, bat, pumpkin, or a moon.

Alternatively, allow the children to 'free paint' with brushes and lots of dark colours on light coloured paper.

Talk about

* Bats: they are not birds with feathers, but flying mammals with fur

* Spiders – who likes them? (And who doesn't?)

* How does it feel to wear a tall, pointed hat?

Stories

* Any of the Meg and Mog stories by Helen Nicoll and Jan Pienkowski (Picture Puffins)

Songs and rhymes

Peter, Peter, pumpkin eater

An easy rhyme to chant or sing.

Peter, Peter, pumpkin eater,
Had a wife and couldn't keep her;
He put her in a pumpkin shell
And there he kept her very well.

Incey Wincey spider

This well-loved little rhyme is fun to do with huge actions!

Incey Wincey spider climbed up the spout.
put left forefinger to right thumb, right forefinger to left thumb, and 'climb'
Down came the rain and washed the spider out,
bring both hands down and out in a sweeping motion
Out came the sunshine and dried up all the rain
lift arms up and spread them out and down
So Incey Wincey spider climbed up the spout again.
make the spider climb up as before

Three little ghostesses

This funny little rhyme can be chanted while playing instruments.

Three little ghostesses
Sitting on postesses,
Eating buttered toastesses,
Greasing their fistesses,
Up to their wristesses –
Oh, what beastesses
To make such feastesses!

What shall I do with my two hands

This easy action song is sung to the tune of 'What shall we do with the drunken sailor?'

Chorus
What shall I do with my two hands?
What shall I do with my two hands?
What shall I do with my two hands
Early in the morning?
   flop your hands about as if you don't know what to do with them

Tap my head and rub my tummy,
Tap my head and rub my tummy,
Tap my head and rub my tummy
Early in the morning.

Chorus

Wiggle my ears and waggle my fingers,
Wiggle my ears and waggle my fingers,
Wiggle my ears and waggle my fingers
Early in the morning.

Chorus

Tap my knees and clap my hands,
Tap my knees and clap my hands,
Tap my knees and clap my hands
Early in the morning.

Creative Activities for the Early Years

Ten fat sausages

Everyone loves to chant this rhyme. Try it kneeling on the floor.

Ten fat sausages sizzling in the pan
  tap knees in time to the chanting
One went POP and the other went BANG!
  clap hands together above head and slap hands down on the floor.

Eight fat sausages sizzling in the pan,
One went POP and the other went BANG!

Six fat sausages…

Four fat sausages…

Two fat sausages…

Try this idea!
At the end of this rhyme open your hands wide and say, 'And then there were no more sausages. Who has eaten all the sausages?' The children love to shout 'Me!'

Other suggestions

*   Little Miss Muffet

*   Supercalifragilisticexpialidocious
    This jolly song from Disney's Mary Poppins *is fun to sing and dance to whilst wearing the witches hats.*

*   Bibbidi-bobbidi boo
    From Disney's Cinderella. *This is an excellent song for dancing along to waving scarves.*

Finish with the Good-bye song on page 8.

Fireworks

Craft activities

Bonfire collage

What you will need
* Black paper (about A4 size) and brown paper
* Different coloured tissue paper in reds, oranges, yellows, etc
* Stars or glitter

What to do
Glue small strips of brown paper near to the bottom of the paper to represent the sticks of the fire. Tear pieces of tissue paper and glue them in layers to the paper, building up the colours. Finish the picture with some stars made from shiny paper or glitter.

Tip
Don't use a lot of glue when you stick tissue paper as it can get a little messy.

Chalk and glitter drawing

What you will need
* Black paper
* Coloured chalks
* Glitter

What to do
Allow the children to use the chalks to make exciting shapes and patterns on the black paper. Then let them add glue and sprinkle glitter onto it to make an easy fireworks picture.

Rockets ⬤⬤

What you will need
* Cardboard tubes (from paper towel rolls or similar)
* Coloured paper
* String
* Small cone shapes from thick paper or thin card
* Streamers (bought or made)

What to do
Cover a cardboard tube with glue and stick on some coloured paper (tissue paper is good for this). You can paint the tubes if you prefer, but wait until they are properly dry before you continue.

Make a small cone shape from thick paper and tape it to the end of the tube. Decorate your rocket with bright colours. Tape a handful of streamers to the inside of the other end of the tube and allow them to fall out behind. Attach some thin string to the centre of the tube (check the balance first) for hanging.

Tip
To make simple streamers quickly, loosely fold thin paper over and over and then cut across the ends in one go. Packs of crepe paper are brilliant for this.

© Barbara Melling
www.brilliantpublications.co.uk

Try this idea!
Make lots of colourful rockets from different sized cardboard rolls and suspend them all in one area to make a fantastic fireworks display, without the bangs!

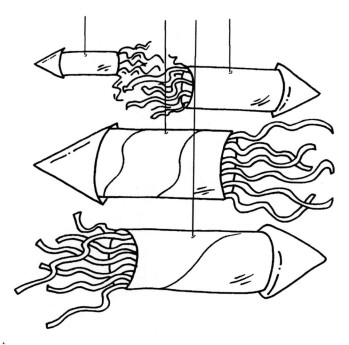

Painting activity

Put out lots of bright paint and sheets of black paper together with brushes or sponge shapes and allow the children to 'free paint' along a fireworks theme.

Budget beater
Buy kitchen sponges with a scouring pad on one side and cut them into simple shapes with scissors. Use the scourer to hold them by.

Talk about

* Bonfire night and fireworks: some of the older children will have been to firework displays – what do they think of them?

* The contrast between light and dark colours; favourite colours

* Loud noises and bangs: do the children like them or not? Think of things that make loud noises

Stories

* *There's a Monster in my House* a lift-the-flap book by Philiip Hawthorn, Jenny Tyler and Stephen Cartwright (Usbourne Publishing)

* *The Smelly Book* by Babette Cole (Red Fox)

Songs and rhymes

Clap your hands, everyone together

This song has lots of actions and movement, and children will love it!

Clap your hands, everyone together,
Clap your hands while the music goes round.
Clap your hands, getting it together,
Clap your hands, stand up, sit down.

Nod your head, everyone together…

Wave your arms, everyone together…

Tap your knees, everyone together…

Stamp your feet, everyone together…

Other suggestions

* Twinkle, twinkle, little star

* Ten fat sausages (see page 31)

* Boys and girls come out to play (see page 23)

* Five little men in a flying saucer
  A funny counting song, it can be sung with or without instruments.

Finish with the Good-bye song on page 8.

Clowns

Craft activities

Biscuit faces

What you will need
* Plain round biscuits
* Icing
* A selection of small decorations, such as tiny sweets, hundreds and thousands, currants

What to do
Spread white or coloured icing on the biscuit and decorate with currants or sweets to look like a clown's funny face.

Try this idea!
Tubes of coloured icing and gel make less mess but aren't quite so much fun.

Tip
Encourage the children to save their biscuit faces until snack time.

Hanging clown

What you will need
* Thin card
* Photocopiable clown template (page 132)
* Butterfly clips (paper fasteners)

What to do
Cut the clown's body and arms out from thin card. Decorate both pieces appropriately with silly trousers, bright buttons and a funny face. Join them together in the centre of the body with a butterfly clip, which can be disguised as a button. Punch a hole at the top and thread some string through so that you can hang the clown.

Tip
Fix the butterfly clip loosely to allow the arms to move.

Clown mask

What you will need
* Paper plates
* String, wool or thin elastic
* Bits and pieces to decorate

What to do
Cut round the edge of the paper plate to create the outline you want. You could have a bald head, tufts of hair, a bow tie, and so on. Cut out eye holes. Brightly colour in the face. Punch a hole on either side and tie the strings through.

Tip
Remember children's eyes are closer together than those of an adult.

Try this idea!
Glue on some cotton wool to make hair. Cut out a hole for the nose and glue on a section of an egg box. Colour the nose bright red.

© Barbara Melling
www.brilliantpublications.co.uk

Painting activity

Cut paper into funny tall hats and decorate with paint.

Try this idea!
Make pom-poms down the front with cotton wool or milk bottle tops. Use the paint as glue.

Talk about

* Has anyone ever seen a clown?

* What kind of things make us laugh?

* What does it feel like, wearing the masks?

Stories

* *Millie's BIG Surprise* by Gerald Rose (Anderson Press)

* *Sometimes I Like to Curl Up in a Ball* by Vicki Churchill and Charles Fuge (Sterling Publishing)

Songs and rhymes

Circus men

This rhyme is said rhythmically or chanted.

Circus men are very funny,
They do this when skies are sunny,
Oompah, dumpah,
Turn around and bumpah.

Stand in pairs and clap alternate hands together for first two lines. Clap together high on Oompah, *clap together low on* Dumpah. *Turn around and bump bottoms together on* Bumpah.

Here we go, Looby Loo

This well-known song is best sung with everyone standing up in a circle.

Chorus
Here we go, Looby Loo,
Here we go, Looby Light,
Here we go, Looby Loo,
All on a Saturday night.

You put one arm in, you put one arm out,
You shake it a little, a little,
And turn yourself about.

Chorus

You put one leg in...

You put your whole self in...

Everyone holds hands and skips round for the chorus. Do the actions for the verses and finish with a chorus.

Other suggestions

* Flippy floppy hands (see page 20)

* There was a crooked man

* If you're happy and you know it (see page 73)

* Nellie the elephant
  The best song to go with marching, instruments or dancing. Lots of CDs and tapes have this.

Finish with the Good-bye song on page 8.

Craft activities

Calendar

What you will need
* Thin card (A4 size)
* Calendar dates (inexpensive and available from shops and pre-school catalogues)
* Ribbon or thin string (for hanging)

What to do
Place the A4 card 'portrait' view and glue the calendar dates near to the bottom. Punch two holes in the centre at the top and thread the ribbon through making a loop ready for hanging. Decorate the card.

Try this idea!
Allow the children to draw their own designs or pictures, either straight onto the card or first onto paper which can be stuck on later.

Try this idea!
Children's hand prints or hand silhouettes are simple to do and make a lovely record for that year.

These simple calendars make lovely Christmas presents for the children to give.

Salt dough tree decorations 1

What you will need
* 300g plain flour
* 300g salt
* 200ml water
* 1 tablespoon oil
* Pastry cutters (optional)
* Rolling pin
* Large bowl
* Skewer

What to do
Mix together the flour, salt, water and oil in a large bowl until it forms a soft dough (add a little more water if needed). Tip onto a floured board or table and gently knead by hand until it is smooth and elastic. Divide the dough into about 10 equal lumps. Set out pastry cutters and rolling pins and allow the children to make shapes with the dough. Use a skewer or cocktail stick to make a small hole near the top of each shape (not too near the edge) to allow them to be hung up.

Tip
About 1.5cm is a good thickness for the dough shapes: too thin and they will snap when cooked, too thick and they will not cook properly.

Place all the dough shapes on to a lightly greased baking sheet and bake at 180°C/350°F or gas mark 4 for 20 minutes.

Tip
If you have no cooking facilities where you meet, perhaps one person could take all the dough shapes home and bring them back cooked the following week, ready for decoration. Initials can be drawn on the backs for identification.

Creative Activities for the Early Years © Barbara Melling
www.brilliantpublications.co.uk

Try this idea!

Make some fridge magnets. Buy small magnets (very cheaply from pre-school catalogues) and glue them on the back once the cooked dough is cooled. You won't need to make the holes for the ribbon.

Tip

Keep the shapes small and light or the magnets won't hold.

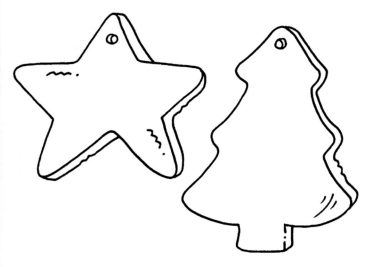

Christmas mobile ⬤ ⬤ ⬤

What you will need
* ✳ Wire coat hangers
* ✳ Tinsel
* ✳ Thin string or wool
* ✳ Photocopiable Christmas template (page 133)
* ✳ Thick paper or card
* ✳ Glitter

What to do
Before the session cut out some simple Christmas shapes from thick paper or thin card.

Choose four or five shapes and decorate them on both sides. Make a small hole in the top and thread through a piece of wool for hanging. Attach different lengths to each of the shapes.

Take the coat hanger and, starting at the hook, wrap the tinsel all the way around it. Secure the tinsel with sticky tape. Hang the shapes from the bottom of the hanger and hang the whole thing up!

Painting activity

Hand-print Christmas tree. Put out brushes and saucers of different greens (mix some with white and some with a little black for various shades). Encourage everyone (adults and children) to paint the palms of their hands and to press them, fingers spread out, onto white paper. When the hand prints are dry, cut them out. Collect as many prints as possible, both left and right hands.

From a large sheet of paper or smaller sheets taped together, cut out a large triangular tree shape to be the pattern – make it large enough to decorate and look good, but not so large you run out of prints. For a tree about 120cm high and 100cm across at the bottom you need about 20 adult prints. Starting at the bottom of the tree pattern, stick rows of prints to the paper, fingers pointing down. Place them fairly close together and with each row slightly overlapping the last. Use the adult prints for the first few rows, smaller prints as you work up the tree, and if you have any baby prints, save them for the top!

Add a trunk and a pot and hang the tree on the wall. Decorate with tinsel and stars for a lovely homemade Christmas tree.

Try this idea!

Hang the bare tree pattern with the trunk and pot on the wall to start with and build up the prints over a few weeks. Encourage everyone to help decorate it.

Talk about

* Christmas! Older children may remember last years, but it will be a new experience for the younger ones.

Stories

* *Mog's Christmas* by Judith Kerr (Harper Collins Children's Books)

* *Happy Christmas Maisy* a lift-the-flap book by Lucy Cousins (Walker Books)

Songs and rhymes

Father Christmas

This little rhyme is sung to the tune of Frère Jacques and can be sung as a round.

Father Christmas, Father Christmas,
He got stuck, he got stuck,
Coming down the chimney, coming down the
chimney.
What bad luck, what bad luck!

Jingle bells

Everyone loves this favourite, which is fun to sing accompanied by bells.

Dashing through the snow in a one-horse open sleigh,
O'er the hills we go, laughing all the way.
Bells on bob tails ring, making spirits light,
Oh what fun it is to sing a sleighing song tonight!

Jingle bells, jingle bells, jingle all the way
Oh what fun it is to ride in a one-horse open
sleigh.
Jingle bells, jingle bells, jingle all the way
Oh what fun it is to ride in a one-horse open
sleigh.

Other suggestions

* Twinkle, twinkle, little star
  Don't forget to get the bells out when you sing this song

* Little Jack Horner

* Santa Clause is coming to town
  This is a great song for dancing along to with scarves and can be found on many Christmas tapes and CD's

* Rudolph the Red-Nosed Reindeer
  Another well-loved favourite, perfect for singing along to, accompanying with instruments, or dancing to with scarves. It can be found on many Christmas CDs and tapes.

* Winter wonderland *and* Rockin' robin
  Both these excellent dancing songs are found on many tapes and CDs.

Finish with the Good-bye song on page 8.

Craft activities

Christmas wreath

What you will need
* Large paper plates
* Green and red tissue paper
* Silver foil cake cases (mince pie cases are excellent)
* Red ribbon

What to do
Make two holes in the top of the plate, thread some ribbon through and make a loop for hanging. Scrunch up pieces of green tissue paper and glue them onto the plate, covering it all except the centre. Snip the edge of a silver foil cake case and bend into a flower shape. Glue the bottom of the case to the centre of the plate. Tie some ribbon into a bow or scrunch up some red tissue paper and glue it inside the cake case (the ribbon can hang out). Tear off small pieces of red tissue, scrunch them up and glue them amongst the green to add some berries.

Hang your finished Christmas wreath on an inside door or in a window for a festive start to the season.

Snowman pictures

What you will need
* A4 sheets of coloured paper
* Cotton wool

What to do
Cut a paper circle about 15cm across for the body and another about 7cm across for the head.

Tip ☆
Draw round a saucer and the inside of a large roll of sticky tape.

Place the A4 paper 'portrait' view and glue the body and head on to it. Cover the snowman with cotton wool and finish him with a hat, a face, buttons and a scarf.

Salt dough tree decorations 2

What you will need
* Baked salt dough decorations (from Christmas 1)
* Paint
* Glitter
* Ribbon

© Barbara Melling
www.brilliantpublications.co.uk

What to do

Make sure everyone has the dough shape they made in the previous session. Allow the children to paint and decorate both sides of their shapes. When dry, thread some ribbon through the hole in the top and make a loop for hanging.

Try this idea!

Thread lots of similar sized shapes onto a long ribbon to make a garland of Christmas decorations.

Painting activity

Continue with the hand-print Christmas tree from Christmas 1. Add decorations, and paint squares, rectangles and circles to stick around the pot for presents.

Cut some large simple Christmas tree shapes from paper and allow the children to paint their own Christmas trees.

Talk about

* Has anyone got a Christmas tree at home?

* Decorations, presents, food, etc; there's lots to talk about

* Have any of the children ever seen snow? What is it like... Cold, wet, white, pretty?

Try this idea!

For a spendid garland, tape a row of Christmas trees by their tops to a thin strip of coloured paper or a length of string.

Stories

* *Happy Christmas Ginger!* by Jakki Wood (Picture Lions)

* *Jingle Bells, Santa's Tune* – a musical storybook by Deborah Campbell-Todd (Brown Watson)

* *The Snowman* by Raymond Briggs Many different versions are available.

Songs and rhymes
We wish you a merry Christmas

This is a perfect Christmas song and can be found on most Christmas tapes and CDs for children.

We wish you a merry Christmas,
We wish you a merry Christmas,
We wish you a merry Christmas
And a happy new year.

Chorus

Good tidings we bring to you and your kin,
We wish you a merry Christmas
And a happy new year.

We all love figgy pudding,
We all love figgy pudding,
We all love figgy pudding
So bring some out here.

Chorus

And we won't go until we've got some,
And we won't go until we've got some,
And we won't go until we've got some
So bring some out here.

Chorus

Christmas is coming

This little rhyme is fun to say while playing instruments.

Christmas is coming, the geese are getting fat,
Please put a penny in the old man's hat.
If you haven't got a penny a ha'penny will do.
If you haven't got a ha'penny, God bless you!

Other suggestions

* Father Christmas (see page 38)

* Jingle bells (see page 38)

* Twinkle, twinkle, little star

* Rudolph the red-nosed reindeer

* Let it snow, let it snow, let it snow
  Brilliant song to dance to with or without instruments or scarves. Can be found on many Christmas tapes and CDs.

* Rockin' around the Christmas tree
  This well-known song is great fun to dance to and can be found on many tapes and CDs.

Finish with the Good-bye song on page 8.

Craft activities

Christmas cards

What you will need
* A4 sheets of thin card
* Christmas shapes for decoration
* Glitter, tinsel

What to do
Before the session, cut some Christmas shapes to fit the cards (stars, trees, stockings, and so on).

Fold the card in half to make a card. Stick one shape onto the front and decorate with tinsel, glitter and coloured paper. (Use cotton wool to decorate Father Christmas.) Include a message inside and write your name or add a decoration.

Try this idea!
Cut a simple Christmas shape out of the front of the card, leaving a neat hole. Open the card and glue a piece of paper or cellophane over the hole. Close the card and decorate the front.

Window lanterns

What you will need
* Black paper
* Photocopiable lantern template (page 134)
* Coloured tissue paper

What to do
Before the session, cut out lantern shapes from black paper using the template.

Cut pieces of tissue paper a little larger than the panels of the lantern. Spread glue on the back of the lantern and stick the tissue over the holes.

Try this idea!
To show the lanterns off put them up in a window and allow the light to shine through the coloured tissue.

Candles

What you will need
* Cardboard tubes about 10cm long
* Orange, yellow and red tissue paper
* Thin card

What to do
Colour the cardboard tube brightly. Cut a circle from the card approximately 12cm across. Tape the tube upright in the centre of the card circle.

Tip
One way of doing this is to put some scrunched-up sticky tape into the end of the tube. Place the end on the card and press the sticky tape down with a pencil.

Push some scrunched-up tissue into the top of the tube and gently tease some out for the flame. Cut a strip of card about 10 x 2cm. Forming it into a loop, attach it to the card circle and the bottom of the tube as the candle holder. Decorate the candle and holder with glitter.

Try this idea!
Curl some ribbon or Christmas tape by pulling it over the blade of a pair of scissors, and arrange it around the bottom of the candle.

Painting activity

Snowflakes: put out sheets of black or dark blue paper and small paper doilies. Brush white paint through the holes in the doilies onto the paper beneath. Carefully remove the doily to reveal a beautiful snowflake, which can be cut out if you wish.

Try this idea!
Sprinkle glitter over the paint while it is wet for a sparkling snowflake.

Talk about

* How we like to send Christmas cards to our friends and families at this time of the year

* How presents can be as much fun to give as to receive

* Christmas

Stories

* *Get Busy This Christmas* by Stephen Waterhouse (Bloomsbury)

* *Maisy's Christmas Eve* by Lucy Cousins (Walker Books)

Songs and rhymes

* We wish you a merry Christmas

* Jingle bells

* Father Christmas

* Twinkle, twinkle, little star

* Little Jack Horner

* Rudolph the red-nosed reindeer

* Santa Clause is coming to town

* Let it snow, let it snow, let it snow

* Rockin' round the Christmas tree

Details of these songs can be found in the two previous Christmas sessions.

Finish with the Good-bye song on page 8.

© Barbara Melling
www.brilliantpublications.co.uk

Christmas party

The secret of a good party is to be organised! Have plenty to do and try to avoid lots of waiting around.

Very young children like simple games and toys so bring a few toys for the under-threes to play with. For a party of mixed ages up to five, here are some ideas.

Craft activity

Party hats

You may want an art activity to start the party. Prepare some paper or thin card for the hats in advance by cutting in along one edge into different shapes. Place the hats together with lots of tinsel, shiny paper, cellophane, stars and cotton wool and let everyone decorate their own party hat. When ready fit them around the children's heads and join with tape.

Tip

This activity engages the children as soon as they arrive so there is no having to wait for latecomers before you can start.

Games

What's the time, Mr Wolf?

This is a great favourite with young children.

One person, the 'wolf', stands at one end of the room with their back to the others. The rest stand at the other end and call out 'What's the time, Mr Wolf?' The wolf, not turning round, calls out a time – for example, 'Three o'clock' and the children take three steps towards him. They ask again and the wolf replies with a different time – for example 'Seven o'clock' – and the children take seven steps towards the wolf. This continues until the wolf calls out 'DINNER TIME!' whereupon he turns round and chases the children back to the start, trying to catch one on the way. The one he catches is now the wolf.

The snowman's in his den

This is a Christmas variation of the 'Farmer's in his den' (see page 47 for the music).

Everyone joins hands and forms a circle and the 'snowman' is chosen to stand in the middle. Everyone in the circle walks round the snowman, singing:

The snowman's in his den,
The snowman's in his den,
E I addy O,
The snowman's in his den.

The snowman wants a wife…
   the snowman chooses someone from the circle to join him in the middle

The wife wants a child…
the wife chooses someone to join them in the middle

The child wants a nurse…
the child chooses someone

The nurse wants a dog…
the nurse chooses someone

We all clap the dog…
everyone claps for the last verse

Pass the parcel

This well-known game is loved by children of all ages.

Try this idea!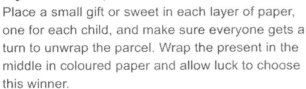
Place a small gift or sweet in each layer of paper, one for each child, and make sure everyone gets a turn to unwrap the parcel. Wrap the present in the middle in coloured paper and allow luck to choose this winner.

Stories

You may wish to have a story at the party as they can be a useful way of diverting the children while the food is being set out, especially if space is limited.

Try this idea!
Although it's not a Christmas book, if you are playing 'What's the time, Mr. Wolf?' a funny book to read is:

* *That's the Time Grandma Wolf?* by Ken Brown (Anderson Press)

Party food

If possible set the food out on tables so the children can sit down to eat. It is easier to manage like this, and more of an occasion for the children.

One way of organising the food is to ask everyone to bring something in. Perhaps make a list, or send home requests to avoid everyone bringing the same thing.

Remember that young children do not eat great quantities so small plates of different types of party food are usually the best idea. You could try:

* Tiny sandwiches (cut into shapes)

* Cucumber sticks and cherry tomatoes

* Biscuits and small cakes (avoid nuts)

* Mandarin segments

* Seedless grapes

* Crisps

* Small sausages and cubes of cheese (avoid cocktail sticks)

Don't forget to provide water as one of the drinks, as lots of children prefer it.

Try this idea!
Put a Christmas cracker, some streamers or a 'tooter' at each place.

Presents from Santa!

You cannot have a Christmas party without presents from Santa.

A few weeks before the party buy a small present for each child and wrap it up. If the presents are individual do not forget to name them! If funds are more limited, ask each parent for a contribution. This is a good idea if some parents are bringing siblings along, as of course they too will require a present. The presents do not have to cost a lot, but try to wrap them nicely.

Some groups may be lucky enough to have a kind volunteer dress up as Santa to come along to hand out the presents, but don't worry if you have no-one to do this. Put all the presents into a large sack (a brightly coloured Christmas sack if possible) and keep it out of sight of the children.

Towards the end of the party sit everyone down quietly. Introduce Santa or explain that he is very busy at this time of year, making toys and getting his sleigh ready, but he has not forgotten their party and has sent a sack full of presents. Lastly, hand out the parcels.

Tip
Make sure you have a spare present, just in case!

Try this idea!
When the children are sitting quietly, Santa (or someone else) can jingle some bells outside the room to herald the arrival of the presents.

Songs and rhymes

* The okey cokey
  OK, so it's not a Christmas song, but children of all ages still love it and it's perfect for a party!

Tip
Don't bother with 'right arm', 'left leg' and so on — just sing 'one arm' and 'one leg'.

* Jingle bells (see page 38)

* Father Christmas (see page 38)

* We wish you a merry Christmas (see page 41)

Finish with the Good-bye song on page 8.

Craft activities

Toy box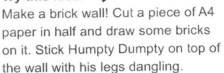

What you will need
* Photocopiable toy box template (page 135)
* Thick paper or thin card
* Lots of pictures of toys (from old catalogues and magazines)

What to do
Before the session, cut out toy box shapes from the card using the template.

The children choose their favourite toys and stick them on. Have lots of pictures for a lovely full toy box.

Humpty Dumpty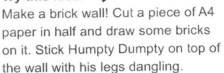

What you will need
* Thick paper
* Thin string or wool (for hanging)

What to do
Cut a large egg shape (at least 15cm high) from the thick paper. Cut two strips from the paper approximately 30 x 3cm. Fold the strips up into a fan shape (alternate folds), with about 3cm between each fold. Attach one end of the strips to the bottom of the egg for the legs. Cut two boot shapes from paper and attach them to the other end of the legs.

Humpty Dumpty is ready for decorating. Add a face, a belt and buckle, arms, and a hat. Tie a loop of string to the top for hanging.

Try this idea!
Make a brick wall! Cut a piece of A4 paper in half and draw some bricks on it. Stick Humpty Dumpty on top of the wall with his legs dangling.

Toy boat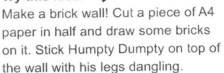

What you will need
* Thick paper or thin card
* Straws

What to do
Cut a boat shape from the card (or have these cut out ready for the session) and attach a straw upright in the centre for a mast. Cut a triangle and tape it to the straw, for the sail. Decorate the boat and sail and add a flag to the top of the mast. Attach another straw along the bottom of the boat with a length sticking out to hold. Pretend the boat is sailing along by holding the straw.

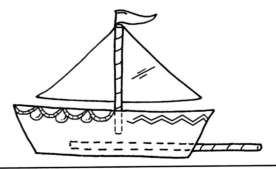

Painting activity

Put out different coloured sheets of paper, paints and brushes and allow the children to 'free paint' as many paintings as they wish.

Talk about

*   The children's favourite toys or Christmas presents

*   Nursery rhymes: Humpty Dumpty; Row, row, row the boat (page 8)

Stories

*   *The Toy Maker* by Martin Waddell and Terry Milne (Walker Books)

*   *Mary's Tiger* by Rex Harley (Orchard Books)

*   *Tatty Ratty* by Helen Cooper (Corgi Childrens)

Songs and rhymes

Humpty Dumpty

This well-known nursery rhyme is fun if the adults sit on the floor with their knees pulled up as the wall so that the children can sit on top. When Humpty Dumpty has a great fall, the adults drop their knees down to the floor.

Humpty Dumpty sat on a wall,
Humpty Dumpty had a great fall,
All the King's horses and all the King's men
Couldn't put Humpty together again.

Put your finger on your head

This funny action song is sung to the tune of 'If you're happy and you know it clap your hands'.

Put your finger on your head, on your head,
Put your finger on your head, on your head,
Put your finger on your head, tell me is it green or red?
Put your finger on your head, on your head.

Put your finger on your nose…
…leave it there until it grows…

Put your finger on your cheek…
…leave it there about a week…

Put your finger on your ear…
…leave it there about a year…

Put your finger on your finger, on your finger,
Put your finger on your finger, on your finger,
Put your finger on your finger, on your finger,
  on your finger,
Put your finger on your finger, on your finger.

For the last verse climb your fingers higher and higher in the air as you put them on top of each other.

Other suggestions

*   Clap your hands, everyone together (see page 33)

*   A sailor went to sea, sea, sea

*   Supercalifragalisticexpialidocious *From Disney's* Mary Poppins.

Rain

Craft activities

'It's raining' collage ◐

What you will need
* Paper
* Photocopiable rainy day template (page 136)
* Silver paper or foil
* Glitter (optional)

What to do
Before the session, cut out lots of rainy day shapes.

Allow the children to create their own collage by decorating the shapes and sticking them onto the paper. Silver paper or foil can be cut or torn into puddle shapes and also used as splashes and raindrops. Glitter can add an extra sparkle!

Rain cloud ◐◐

What you will need
* Card (cereal box card is perfect)
* Strips of bubble wrap
* Silver paper of foil
* Thin string (for hanging)

What to do
Cut a cloud shape about 20cm across from thick card and colour it grey (paint covers well). Cut the bubble wrap and silver paper into thin strips of different lengths and attach them to the bottom of the cloud (at the back) for the rain. Add a loop of string to the top of the cloud for hanging.

Weather chart ◐◐◐

What you will need
* Thin coloured card (A4)
* Photocopiable weather chart template (page 137)
* Plain paper (A4)
* String or wool for hanging

What to do
Photocopy the window template onto thin card. Carefully cut along the lines. Turn the card over and bend the squares out to make six hinged flaps. This is better done in advance and as neatly as possible.

Place the plain paper underneath the card and lightly pencil around the inside of the open squares. The children can then draw pictures representing six different types of weather in the squares – for example, a kite, a snowman, an umbrella, a fluffy cloud, a sandcastle, a flash of lightning. The more colours the better.

Place the card over the paper, matching the squares with the pictures, turn both pieces over and secure them together with sticky tape. Label the flaps with the appropriate type of weather. If the flaps don't stay shut attach a small sticky label (or part of one) to the edge. Add a loop of string to the top of the chart for hanging. You could even decorate around the edge.

Use the chart to show the day's weather. Open the appropriate door or doors each time.

Painting activity

Rainbows! Put out plenty of paper and the colours of the rainbow – red, orange, yellow, green, blue, dark purple and light purple.

Talk about

* Different types of weather and which the children prefer

* The right clothes for the weather – what we wear in the rain, in the sun…

* Rain and what it does: waters the plants, makes puddles to splash in…

* Rainbows. Has anyone seen one? Explain how they appear when there is rain and sunshine

Stories

* *Tommee's Book of Colours* by Linda Groark (Kingfisher Books)

* *The First Rainbow: the story of Noah's Ark* by Sue Box and Susie Poole (Lions Children's Books)

* *Oi! Get Off Our Train* by John Burningham (Red Fox)

Songs and rhymes

It's raining, it's pouring

This is a very well-known rhyme. It can be chanted with instruments or said as a round.

It's raining, it's pouring,
The old man is snoring,
He went to bed and banged his head
And wouldn't get up in the morning.

I hear thunder

This song is sung to the tune of 'Frère Jacques.'
Make up some simple actions to accompany it.

I hear thunder, I hear thunder,
Hark, don't you? Hark, don't you?
Pitter patter raindrops, pitter patter raindrops,
I'm wet through. I'm wet through.

I see blue skies, I see blue skies,
Way up high, way up high.
Hurry up the sunshine, hurry up the sunshine,
I'll soon dry. I'll soon dry.

Other suggestions

✻ Incey Wincey spider (see page 30)

✻ Somewhere over the rainbow
This lovely song from The Wizard of Oz *is ideal for dancing to with scarves.*

✻ I can sing a rainbow
This gentle lullaby, perfect for calming everyone down, can be found on many tapes and CDs.

✻ The sun has got his hat on
This jolly song can be found on many children's tapes and CDs.

Finish with the Good-bye song on page 8.

Craft activities

Chinese lantern

What you will need
* A4 paper
* String or wool

What to do
First decorate the whole of the paper with patterns or Chinese designs. Place the paper 'landscape' view and fold it in half to make a long thin rectangle. Cut snips 3cm apart and 6cm long along the length of the fold, starting and finishing 3cm from each edge.

Open the paper out. Form it into a cylinder shape and tape (or staple) the shorter edges together, overlapping by 3cm. Attach the string to the top to make a loop for hanging. Gently press the lantern down, allowing the side slits to bulge outwards.

Try this idea!
For a festive look thread all the lanterns onto a length of string and suspend them across the room.

Chinese stick puppets

Fish

What you will need
* Photocopiable fish template (page 138)
* Thin card
* Pea stick

What to do
Photocopy the fish onto thin card. Decorate it with shiny scales, big eyes and streamers coming from fins, tail and mouth. Attach a pea stick to the bottom half of the fish in the middle. Wave the fish in the air and the streamers will swish around it.

Lion

What you will need
* Photocopiable lion template (page 139)
* Thin card
* Pea stick
* Wool pieces

What to do
Photocopy the lion onto thin card. Decorate it with large eyes and coloured wool for the mane. Attach a pea stick to the bottom half of the lion in the middle and make him pounce and roar.

Safety note
Always be careful when using pea sticks with very small children. Do not leave the sticks loose on the table.

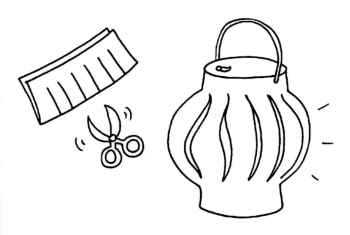

Chinese dragon
puppet ○ ● ○

What you will need
* ✳ Coloured tissue paper
* ✳ Thin card
* ✳ Photocopiable dragon shapes (page 140)
* ✳ Pea sticks
* ✳ Streamers or shiny strips

What to do
Cut a dragon head shape and a tail shape from the thin card and colour. Cut two strips of approximately 4cm wide and 60cm long, each from a different colour tissue paper. Place the ends at right angles to each other and secure with tape. Fold the strips back, one over the other until all the tissue is used and you have a small fat square of tissue. Tape the ends together. Gently pull the folded tissue out for the body. Attach one end of the tissue body to the head and the other to the tail.

Tape one pea stick to the head and one to the tail. Cut streamers or thin strips of shiny paper (or tissue) and attach them to the mouth for firey breath. Hold the pea sticks and make the dragon dance up and down.

Painting activity
Cut potatoes or sponges into Chinese shapes or writing and print onto coloured paper.

Tip
Sponge shapes can be bought very cheaply from shops and pre-school catalogues and last a long time.

Talk about
* ✳ Chinese food. Bring in some Chinese snacks for the children to sample, such as prawn crackers or fortune cookies

* ✳ Chop sticks. Bring some in for the children to try

Stories
* ✳ *Zoe and the Dragon* by Jane Andrews (Piccadilly Press)

* ✳ *The Egg* by M.P. Robertson (Frances Lincoln Publishers)

* ✳ *Ella's Games* by David Bedford and Peter Kavanagh (Scholastic Hippo)

© Barbara Melling
www.brilliantpublications.co.uk

Songs and rhymes

I'm a lion in the forest

Half the group can pretend to be the lion and say the lion line and the other half can reply with the second line.

I'm a lion in the forest and I'm looking for my tea.
Oh, please, Mr Lion… don't eat me!

I'm a lion in the forest, and I must have some meat.
Oh, please, Mr Lion… I'm not the one to eat!

I'm a lion in the forest and I've waited long enough!
Oh, please, Mr Lion… you'll find I'm very tough!

Other suggestions

* Criss cross apple sauce (see page 16)

* One, two, three, four, five (see page 8)

* Put your finger on your head (see page 49)

* Sammy's Safari
   A jolly song for playing along to with instruments or dancing to.

* Puff the magic dragon
   A gentle calming song that makes a lovely lullaby ending for a session. It can be found on many recordings for children.

Finish with the Good-bye song on page 8.

Craft activities

Houses of straw, sticks and bricks

What you will need
* Simple house shapes cut from thick paper
* Straw
* Small sticks or twigs

What to do
Draw a door and windows on three of the house shapes. Glue straw on the first house, including its roof, but avoiding the door and windows. Glue small sticks or twigs on the second house in the same way.

Tip
Use lots of glue and keep the houses flat until they are dry.

For the third house either draw on bricks or cut out rectangles of coloured paper and stick them on. Draw or stick on the roof tiles, using a different colour from the bricks. Colour or decorate the doors and windows on all three houses.

Pig mask

What you will need
* Large paper plate
* Paper or plastic cup
* String

What to do
Cut two eye holes in the plate, remembering that children's eyes are closer together than those of an adult. Colour the paper plate pink.

Cut off the top of the paper cup (slightly less than halfway down) and colour the remaining part pink.

Tip
If using paint for the plate and cup, add a little PVA glue to the paint to stop it flaking off when it's dry.

Cut a hole in the plate for the nose to fit through comfortably and stick the paper cup, upside down, over the top.

Cut two paper ears and colour them pink. Attach them to the top of the mask. Fix two pieces of string to the sides. Add a mouth, nostrils, spots and eyelashes – and your pig mask is finished!

Pig and wolf finger puppets

What you will need
* Thin card
* Photocopiable pig and wolf template (page 141)

What to do
Cut round the animal shapes carefully, cutting two holes near the bottom for fingers. Colour the pig and add a snout, front trotters, spots and a hat. Colour the wolf and add a long nose, big eyes and front paws. Don't draw hind legs on either animal: put your index and middle fingers through the holes to make the hind legs.

Tip
The holes will be smaller and closer together for children's fingers.

Try this idea!
Make three pig finger puppets, one for each house!

Painting activity

Put out lots of sheets of different coloured paper, together with paints and brushes, and allow the children to 'free paint' as many pictures as they wish.

Talk about

* Pigs: where they live, what noise they make, what young pigs are called

* Which house would be the strongest? Which would be the nicest to live in?

* Wolves: they look like dogs, they live in groups called packs in cold countries

Story

* *The Three Little Pigs*
There are hundreds of versions of this favourite fairy tale.

Try this idea!
Encourage the children to wear their masks (some may prefer to have them on top of their heads) for the story and the songs about pigs. Try acting out the story with the masks or finger puppets.

Songs and rhymes

This little piggy went to market

This well-known rhyme is fun to do with the children's toes, but it works just as well on fingers. Tickle the children on the last line.

This little piggy went to market,
This little piggy stayed at home,
This little piggy had roast beef,
This little piggy had none
And this little piggy cried wee, wee, wee,
All the way home.

Dickery, dickery, dare

When saying this little nonsense rhyme jump up from a crouching position then drop back down again.

Dickery, dickery, dare,
The pig flew up in the air;
The man in brown
Soon brought him down,
Dickery, dickery, dare.

Tom, Tom, the piper's son

This well-known nursery rhyme is perfect for accompanying with instruments.

Tom, Tom, the piper's son,
Stole a pig and away did run;
The pig was eat
And Tom was beat
And Tom went howling down the street.

Seven little pigs went to market

Seven little pigs went to market,
One of them fell down,
One of them, he ran away,
And five pigs got to town.

Five little pigs went to market,
One of them fell down,
One of them, he ran away,
And three pigs got to town.

Three little pigs went to market,
One of them fell down,
One of them, he ran away,
And one pig got to town!

Other suggestions

✳ Ten fat sausages (see page 31)

✳ Little green frog song (see page 12)

✳ I went to visit a farm one day
Fun for singing along to or accompanying with instruments.

✳ Old MacDonald (see page 13)
Everyone loves this favourite.

Finish with the Good-bye song on page 8.

Creative Activities for the Early Years

Craft activities

Tip
Do not tighten the butterfly clip too much or the crocodile's jaw will not open and shut smoothly.

Monkey mask

What you will need
* Thin card
* Photocopiable monkey mask (page 142)
* String or wool

What to do
Cut the monkey mask from thin card. Cut out the eye holes and make two small holes either side of the face. Decorate the mask and thread two pieces of string through the holes for tying round your head.

Snake ○○

What you will need
* Large sheets of coloured paper
* Wool

What to do
Draw the biggest circle you can fit onto your paper (at least the size of a dinner plate, much bigger if possible!) Lightly draw around the inside of the circle, making about two or three spirals and ending in the centre with a head shape. (This can all be done in advance.)

Decorate the snake with colours and patterns.

Cut along the lines from the outside to the middle. Attach a piece of wool to the middle of the head (for hanging) and add a forked tongue to the mouth. Suspend the snake away from a wall and it's body will fall in coils.

Crocodile ○○

What you will need
* Thin card
* Photocopiable crocodile shapes (page 143)
* Butterfly clips (paper fasteners)
* Rice

What to do
Cut the crocodile shape and the lower jaw shape from the card. Add details to the crocodile e.g. eyes, scales (small pieces of green paper stuck on). Spread glue along the lower edge of the upper jaw and the upper edge of the lower jaw and pour on the rice grains. Press them into the glue and shake off the excess. These are the crocodile's teeth. Place the lower jaw in place under the crocodile and join them together with a butterfly clip.

Painting activity

Make easy parrots with colourful hand prints. Print them straight onto the paper or cut them out and stick them. Start at the tail and keeping the fingers out arrange the prints in slightly overlapping layers over the head and down the back. Add eyes, a beak and feet on a branch.

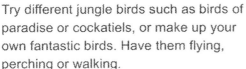

Try this idea!
Try different jungle birds such as birds of paradise or cockatiels, or make up your own fantastic birds. Have them flying, perching or walking.

Talk about

✳ Has anyone seen these animals at the zoo?

✳ Has anyone seen a parrot before?

✳ What do these birds and animals like to eat?

Stories

✳ *Dear Zoo* a lift-the-flap book by Rod Campbell (Campbell Books)

✳ *All Together Now!* a lift-the-flap book by Nick Butterworth (Picture Lions)

✳ *Millie's BIG Surprise* by Gerald Rose (Anderson Press)

Songs and rhymes

Walking in the jungle

This excellent action song is an all time favourite with children! Chant it very rhythmically or make up a simple tune. Ask everyone to kneel on the floor. The leader says the first phrase, the group say the repeat.

Walking in the jungle, walking in the jungle,
tap hands on knees to sound like footsteps

What can you see? What can you see?
shade eyes and search

Can you hear a noise? Can you hear a noise?
cup hand behind ear to 'listen'

What can it be? What can it be?
tap hands on knees

Well, I think it's a TIGER! Grrr, grrr, grrr, grrr.
claw fingers in the air (towards the children) and growl

Well, I think it's a tiger, grrr, grrr, grrr, grrr.
Well, I think it's a tiger, grrr, grrr, grrr, grrr,
Looking for his tea, looking for his tea.
tap hands on knees

Walking in the jungle etc…

Well, I think it's a SNAKE! Sss, sss, sss, sss…
slither hands and arms (towards children) and hiss

Well I think it's a CROCODILE! Snap, snap, snap, snap…
snap arms together (towards the children) and snap
Looking for his tea, looking for his tea,
tap hands on knees
And I hope it isn't me, and I hope it isn't me!

Five little monkeys

Another fantastic action song, that everyone will love. Can be chanted or sung. Don't forget to shout the last line!

Five little monkeys swinging in the tree,
   swing both arms down towards the floor
Along came a crocodile as quiet as can be.
   put your wrists together and hands open
'Ah ha!' said the monkeys, 'you can't catch me.'
   wag your finger
SNAP went the crocodile and ate one for tea!
   snap your hands and arms together

Four little monkeys swinging in the tree…

Three little monkeys…

Two little monkeys…

One little monkey swinging in the tree,
Along came a crocodile quiet as can be.
'Ah ha' said the monkey, 'YOU MISSED ME!'

If you should meet a crocodile

It is easy to act out this rhyme. At the last line shout 'DINNER' and try to 'snap' your arms at the nearest person.

If you should meet a crocodile,
Don't take a stick and poke him;
Ignore the welcome in his smile,
Be careful not to stroke him.
For as he sleeps beside the Nile,
He thinner gets and thinner.
So when ever you meet a crocodile,
He's ready for his DINNER!

Other suggestions

✳   Row, row, row the boat (see page 8)

✳   Pretty polly parrot
   This is a good marching song to play with instruments.

✳   Never smile at a crocodile
   An excellent song to parade round the room to with instruments.

✳   I went to the animal fair
   Fun to dance to with scarves.

Finish with the Good-bye song on page 8.

Jake the snake

Make your hand and arm into a snake that 'sleeps' until the last line, at which it tickles the nearest child.

There once was a snake and his name was Jake,
And he slept in the sun all day.

At night that snake, whose name was Jake,
Slithered and slipped away.

Barbara Melling

Craft activities

Heart collage

What you will need

* Large piece of paper
* Heart shapes – lots of different sizes and colours

What to do

Either keep the paper as it is or cut it into as large a heart shape as you can. Have a pile of heart shapes cut from different paper, magazines, sweet wrappers and so on. Stick your favourites onto the base paper, until you have built up a colourful collage.

Valentine's card

What you will need

* Thin card (A4)
* Red, pink and white fabric heart shapes (use different textures such as felt, velvet, cord and cotton)
* Red, pink and white beads
* Pieces of lace
* Paper doilies
* Glitter
* Shiny paper

Budget beater
Different fabrics and beads can be bought very cheaply from charity shops.

What to do

Fold the card in half. Cut hearts from the shiny paper. Separate the beads into short strings or individual beads. Place all the hearts and beads, together with any thing else you may have found that is pink, red or white on the table. The children will love choosing from the array of hearts, beads and lace to make their own arrangement on their cards. Glue the arrangement down. Complete the card with lots of glitter and your message (or drawing) on the inside.

Children love to make valentine cards for their parents or favourite relatives.

Tip
Some fabrics will need lots of glue to stick, while others will use hardly any!

Safety note
Be careful using beads with very young children. Try to keep the beads on short strings rather than have them loose.

Creative Activities for the Early Years

Heart mobile

What you will need
* Coloured paper
* Wool
* Glitter
* Shredded newspaper or similar

What to do
Before the session, cut two heart shapes at least 12cm long.

If the paper is plain decorate it first. Place the two hearts on top of each other (decorated sides facing out) and staple around the edges to join them together, leaving one side open. Fill the 'pocket' with scrunched-up or shredded paper (newspaper is very good) and complete the staples. Attach a loop of wool to the top for hanging.

Tip
Add any glitter once the heart has been padded.

Cut some smaller hearts (at least two) and decorate them on both sides. Attach wool to the tops and suspend them, one from the padded heart and one below that one.

Try this idea!
The more hearts you make, padded or flat, the longer your mobile will be. Use lots of different colours and sizes.

Painting activity
Put out some heart stencils, either bought or homemade (cereal box card is the best). Use sponge squares to dab on the paint, which can be put out in saucers. Have lots of paper – and stencils of other shapes too.

Talk about
* The different textures of the fabric hearts. What do they feel like? Which is the best?

* People the children love: parents, siblings, grandparents, friends

* Pets and toys the children love

Stories
* *I Love You Blue Kangaroo!* by Emma Chichester Clark (Anderson Press)

* *No Matter What* by Debi Gliori (Bloomsbury)

* *My Mum is Fantastic* by Nick Butterworth (Walker Books)

Songs and rhymes

Roses are red
This well-known rhyme is easy for children to learn, especially with a tickle on the last line!

Roses are red,
Violets are blue,
Sugar is sweet
And so are you.

Wind the bobbin up

This well-known song has lots of actions. Wind your hands round and round for the first line, then pull them apart and clap, wind them the other way for the third line and then follow the actions in the song.

Wind the bobbin up, wind the bobbin up,
Pull, pull, clap, clap, clap.
Wind it back again, wind it back again,
Pull, pull, clap, clap, clap.
Point to the window, point to the door,
Point to the ceiling, point to the floor.
Clap your hands together, one, two, three,
Put your hands upon your knee.

Try this idea!
Sing the song through
three times, slowly at first,
then getting faster and
faster.

Other suggestions

＊ Criss cross apple sauce (see page 16)

＊ Flippy floppy hands (see page 20)

＊ Here we go Looby Loo (see page 35)

＊ I wanna be like you
This song from the Jungle Book *is good for joining in with instruments or dancing to.*

＊ Waterloo
Yes the Abba song - great for bopping around to. Found on many children's CDs.

Finish with the Good-bye song on page 8.

Creative Activities for the Early Years

Mice, mice, mice

Craft activities

Finger mouse

What you will need
* Sugar paper or other stiff paper

What to do
Cut a fat cone shape, nearly the length of your index finger, with two semi circles at the top near the centre (see drawing) for the ears. Roll the paper round to make a cone and secure it. Bend the ears forward. Attach some small paper whiskers and draw some eyes. Slip this on and your finger will become a mouse!

If you wish, you can make a ring of paper to fit behind the head with a tail attached. Usually children's fingers are not big enough for a tail, but you can make one for yourself.

Note
Children's fingers are a lot smaller than adults'.

Tip
For a curly tail, pull the blade of a pair of scissors along the strip of paper.

Try this idea!
Make lots of finger mice and use them to illustrate a story or song.

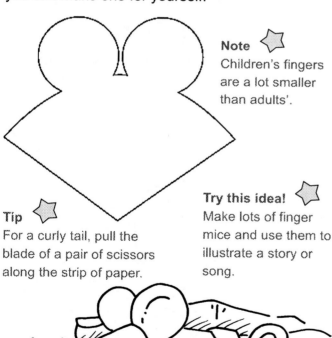

Mouse nose and whiskers

What you will need
* Egg box
* String
* Straws cut into 8cm lengths

What to do
Cut a section out of an egg box and punch a hole in either side of it, near the top edge, then thread some string through. Next glue the straws to the end of the nose for the whiskers. Tape two large paper teeth to the lower edge of the nose. Colour the nose.

Try this idea!
Have fun drawing the nose and whiskers on with face paints for a different mouse face.

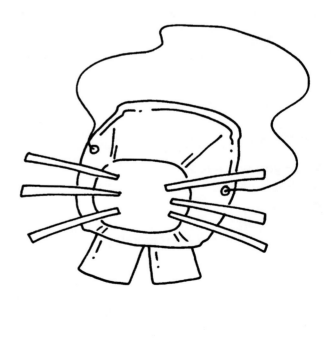

Mouse ears

What you will need

* Cardboard (flattened cereal packets)
* Coloured paper (pink or red, painted or coloured)

What to do

Cut strips of cardboard about 3cm wide and long enough to fit around a child's head. You might need to join two pieces together. For the ears cut out two circles about 12cm across with the bottom cut off. Using coloured paper, cut out smaller ear shapes about 8cm wide and stick them to the cardboard ears. Attach both to the front of the headband with staples or tape. Colour the ears to match the nose (page 65). Fit them round the child's head and join them together.

Tip
Always measure the band around the child's head first before securing. Also, staple outwards so the staple ends do not catch the hair.

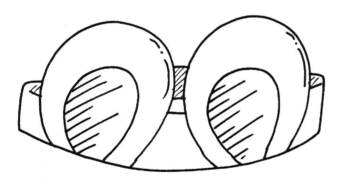

Mouse plaque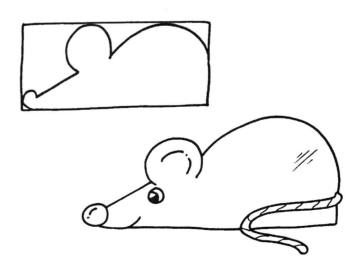

What you will need

* Black card
* String
* Egg box
* Straws cut into short lengths

What to do

Cut a mousehole about 10cm high from black card and punch a hole in the top. Thread some string through and tie into a loop to hang it by. Cut a section from an egg box to make the mouse head and cut two small paper ears.

Glue the egg box and ears to the bottom of the hole, so the mouse is peeping out. Before the glue dries, tie a knot in a piece of string about 8cm long and tuck the knotted end behind the egg box so the string pokes out and looks like a tail. Colour and glue the straws on for whiskers and draw on some eyes.

Hang the finished plaque on the wall or attach it to the skirting board for a lifelike mouse hole!

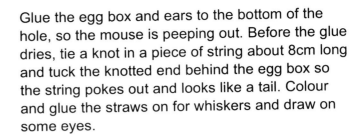

Painting activity

Cut out large, simple mice shapes (side view) for the children to paint. Attach a piece of string or wool for a tail.

Creative Activities for the Early Years
© Barbara Melling
www.brilliantpublications.co.uk

Talk about

* Where mice live – field mice in the country and town mice in towns, in holes and nests

* What mice might like to eat

* What would it be like to be as small as a mouse?

Stories

* *Little Mouse Twitchy Whiskers* by Margaret Mayo and Penny Dann (Orchard Books)

* *Ella's Games* by David Bedford and Peter Kavanagh (Scholastic Children's Press)

* *Little Mouse and the Big Red Apple* by A.H. Benjamin and Gwyneth Williamson (Little Tiger Press)

Songs and rhymes

Hickory dickory dock

Everyone knows this rhyme, but here are a few extra verses. Hold one arm upright from the elbow (the clock) and make the other hand the mouse.

Hickory dickory dock,
The mouse ran up the clock.
The clock struck one,
The mouse ran down,
Hickory dickory dock.
Tick tock, tick tock.

The clock struck two,
The mouse said Boo…

The clock struck three,
The mouse went Weeeeee…

The clock struck four,
There is no more…

Four little field mice fast asleep

Use the fingers of one hand as the mice and the other hand as the owl. Put one finger down at a time. Make up a tune and shout 'SCOOT!'.

Four little field mice fast asleep
All in a huddle, all in a heap,
Along came an owl who gave a hoot,
And one little mouse went SCOOT!

Three little field mice…

Try this idea!
Act out the song with the children wearing their mice ears as the field mice. Choose someone to be the owl.

Five little mice were playing one day

This is another little rhyme that can be acted out or said using fingers.

Five little mice were playing one day,
Dancing about so bright and gay,
Along came a cat so big and tall
And one scampered back to his hole in the wall.

Four little mice…

Other suggestions

* Three blind mice

* Pussy cat, pussy cat, where have you been?

* The work song
  From Walt Disney's Cinderella. *This is an excellent song for accompanying with instruments, or why not pretend to be little mice and scamper around.*

Finish with the Good-bye song on page 8.

Craft activities

Boat collage ○

What you will need
* Paper (at least A4 size)
* Tissue paper (blue and green)
* Cotton wool

What to do
Cut out some simple boat shapes and lighthouses. Use these together with some tissue and cotton wool to create your own picture. Add the details to the boats and have some birds in the sky.

Try this idea!
Stick long strips of blue tissue paper across the paper for the sea. Stick small pieces of scrunched-up green tissue paper on one side for the land. The cotton wool makes fluffy clouds in the sky.

Hanging seagull ◐ ◐

What you will need
* Thin card (at least A3 size)
* Photocopiable seagull template (page 144)
* String or thin elastic

What to do
Fold the card in half and cut a seagull shape from the thin card with the edge of the template along the fold (this can be done in advance). With the fold pointing up, attach the string to the centre of the back in two places to make a loop. Decorate both sides of the seagull and add eyes (some seagulls have black wing and tail tips). Suspend the seagull from the ceiling (add to the loop if you need to) so that it can flap freely.

Try this idea!
If you use elastic to hang it by, gently pull the gull down a little and then let go to see the gull's wings flap.

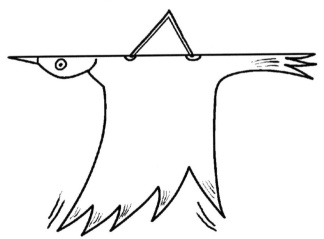

Lighthouse ● ● ●

What you will need
* Large plastic bottle (large fizzy drink bottles are best)
* Coloured paper
* Paper/plastic cup
* Circle of thin card about 8cm across
* Glitter

What to do

Cut three strips of paper 10 x 35cm, two from one colour and one from another colour. Glue these round the bottle, starting from the bottom and working up with alternate colours, leaving no bottle showing between the strips. Glue or tape the upturned plastic cup to the top of the bottle. Cover the circle of thin card with glue and coat with glitter. Attach the circle to the front of the plastic cup as a light. Cut out and decorate a door and a few windows and stick them onto the lighthouse (do not forget to put some round the back).

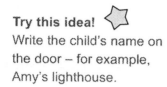

Try this idea!

Write the child's name on the door – for example, Amy's lighthouse.

Painting activity

Stencils of boats and fish (easily obtained from shops or pre-school catalogues) can be put out with rollers or sponges and saucers of paint. Children of all ages and abilities love stencils and sponges.

Tip

Allow the children to smudge the prints or to print one on top of another if they want to – it's part of the creative process!

Talk about

* How lighthouses used to prevent ships from crashing onto the rocks in storms

* Has anyone seen or been inside a lighthouse?

* Has anyone been in a boat or ship? What was it like? Where did they go?

Stories

* *Mr Gumpy's Outing* by John Burningham (Red Fox)

* *Captain Duck* by Jez Alborough (Collins)

* *Fidgety Fish* by Ruth Galloway (Little Tiger Press)

Songs and rhymes

I love to rock in my big red boat

See music on page 70.

I love to rock in my big red boat,
My big red boat, my big red boat,
I love to rock in my big red boat,
Out on the deep blue sea.

My big red boat has two green sails,
Two green sails, two green sails,
My big red boat has two green sails,
Out on the deep blue sea.

So come for a rock in my big red boat,
My big red boat, my big red boat,
So come for a rock in my big red boat,
Out on the deep blue sea.

The big ship sails on the alley alley-o

This well-known song is best sung with everyone standing in a circle.

The big ship sails on the alley alley-o
The alley alley-o, the alley alley-o,
The big ship sails on the alley alley-o
On the last day of September.
    make wavy sea motions with alternate hands

The captain said it'll never never do,
Never never do, never never do,
The captain said it'll never never do
On the last day of September.
    wag your fingers

The big ship sinks to the bottom of the sea,
The bottom of the sea, the bottom of the sea,
The big ship sinks to the bottom of the sea
On the last day of September.
    *raise your arms above your head and bend
    your knees to crouch down*

So we all dip our heads in the deep blue sea,
The deep blue sea, the deep blue sea,
We all dip our heads in the deep blue sea
On the last day of September.
    *standing up, bend at your waist and shake
    your head*

Other suggestions

*   Bobby Shaftoe's gone to sea (see page 8)

*   Seagull, seagull, sit on the shore (see page 118)

*   A sailor went to sea, sea, sea
    Excellent for instruments.

*   Bobbing up and down like this
    Fun to bob up and down to.

*   Under the sea
    From Disney's Little Mermaid. *Brilliant for
    dancing to.*

Finish with the Good-bye song on page 8.

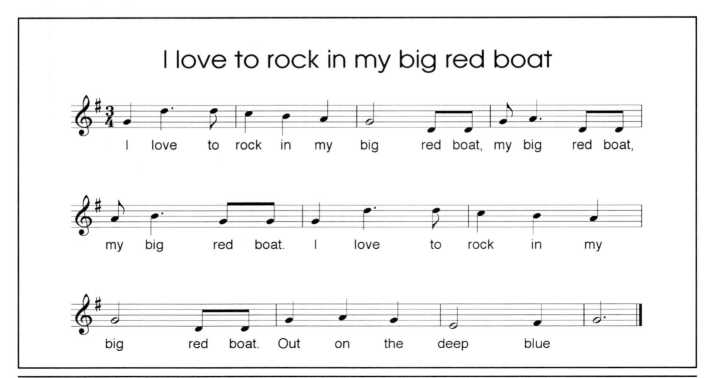

I love to rock in my big red boat

I love to rock in my big red boat, my big red boat, my big red boat. I love to rock in my big red boat. Out on the deep blue

Creative Activities for the Early Years

Mother's Day

Craft activities

Mother's Day card ⊙ ⊙

What you will need
* Thin card (A4)
* Coloured paper
* Tea bag

What to do
Fold the card in half. Cut out a simple cup shape and a simple saucer shape (side view) and decorate them. Spread glue around the edge of the cup, leaving the top and the inside free, and stick it onto the card. Stick the saucer under the cup. Decorate the rest of the card and put a message or drawing inside. Wait until the glue is completely dry then pop the teabag into the cup.

Photograph present ⊙ ⊙

What you will need
* Photograph of yourself
* Thin card (A4 size)
* Ribbon or string
* Coloured paper
* Rice, grains, etc (optional)

What to do
Cut the coloured paper to fit the thin card, leaving a margin of about 75mm all around. Stick the photograph in the top part of the paper and create some painted hand prints or finger prints in the bottom half. Glue the paper to the card. Punch two holes near the top of the card and thread the ribbon through, making a loop for hanging. Finally decorate the margin by sticking on glitter or grains (or both) or draw your own pattern.

Tip ☆
Ask everyone a few weeks before to bring in a photo of themselves.

Try this idea! ☆
This is a lovely present to give to Grandma on Mother's Day!

Peppermint creams in a basket ⚫⚫⚫

This will make a lovely present for Mother's Day.

What you will need

* Icing sugar
* Peppermint essence
* Large bowl
* Water
* Coloured paper (A4 size)
* Greaseproof paper (or similar)

What to do

Put 340g of icing sugar into a large bowl and add a few drops of peppermint essence (the more you use the stronger the taste). Add the water a few drops at a time and mix well before adding further or the mixture will be too runny. (If this happens add more icing sugar.) Knead the mixture together until you have a stiff ball of icing. Dust a surface with icing sugar, divide the mixture into 16 small balls and allow the children to shape them.

Tip
Crushed mints make a perfect substitute for peppermint essence.

Cut a piece of coloured paper in half and place it 'landscape' view. Cut a strip 3cm wide off from one of the short sides and put this to one side. Make a fold 4cm wide along each of the four edges of the paper, folding them over towards the middle, then open the paper out again. Cut along both horizontal folds from the outside edge to the vertical fold to make a flap at each corner. Decorate the basket.

Tip
Cut out the baskets in advance. They're easy and don't have to be exact.

Fold the sides up and overlap the flaps. Staple or tape them in place. Staple the strip cut off earlier to each side of the basket for a handle. Put some greaseproof paper inside and carefully fill with the peppermint creams.

Tip
Don't use tissue paper instead of greaseproof, as the colour runs!

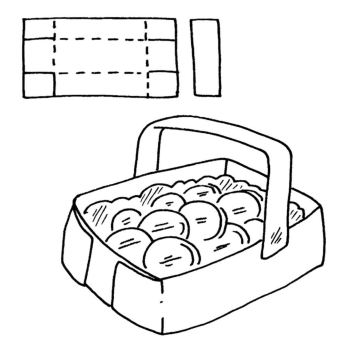

Painting activity

Put out lots of paper and paint and allow the children to paint their own pictures.

Talk about

* Mummy: what she likes and dislikes

* What the children like best about their mums

Stories

* *My Mum is Fantastic* by Nick Butterworth (Walker Books)

* *Five Minutes' Peace* by Jill Murphy (Walker Books)

* *Big Bears Can!* by David Bedford and Gaby Hansen (Little Tiger Press)

Songs and rhymes

Polly put the kettle on

This well-known rhyme is perfect for playing along to with instruments.

Polly put the kettle on,
Polly put the kettle on,
Polly put the kettle on, we'll all have tea.

Sukey take it off again,
Sukey take it off again,
Sukey take it off again, they've all gone away.

Father and Mother and Uncle John

The child sits on the adult's knee. Collapse knees for father and mother falling off, but jog on and on after that.

Father and Mother and Uncle John
Went to market one by one;
Father fell off…!
Mother fell off…!
But Uncle John went on and on,
And on and on and on.

If you're happy and you know it, clap your hands

This well-known song can be found on many recordings.

If you're happy and you know it clap your hands,
(clap, clap)
If you're happy and you know it clap your hands,
(clap, clap)
If you're happy and you know it,
And you really want to show it,
If you're happy and you know it clap your hands.
(clap, clap)

If you're happy and you know it nod your head…
(nod, nod)

If you're happy and you know it stamp your feet…
(stamp, stamp)

If you're happy and you know it shout 'WE ARE'!…
(shout 'WE ARE!')

Other suggestions

✳ Old Mother Hubbard

✳ There was an old woman who lived in a shoe

✳ Flippy floppy hands (see page 20)

✳ She'll be coming round the mountain
   This is a great song for playing instruments and marching along to. Many recordings have this tune.

✳ A spoonful of sugar
   An excellent dancing song, with scarves.

Finish with the Good-bye song on page 8.

Springtime

Craft activities

Lambs

What you will need
* Thin card
* Photocopiable lamb template (page 145)
* Cotton wool
* Green tissue paper

What to do
Cut a lamb shape from the card. Fold along the back to allow it to stand. Staple or tape the tail together and do the same with the nose. Cover the lamb with glue and stick on the cotton wool. If you wish, colour the face and legs black before folding.

Cut a rectangle from card approximately 16cm x 10cm for the base. Fold under about 1cm at each of the lamb's feet and glue them to the base. Glue on scrunched-up pieces of green tissue paper for a grassy field.

Planting sunflower seeds

What you will need
* Sunflower seeds
* Soil
* Small plant pots/yoghurt pots
* Small trowel or spoon
* Labels or paper
* Plastic sheet

What to do
In a quiet corner of the room, set out the soil, trowel, pots and seeds on the sheet. When the seeds have been planted make sure each pot has a label attached (or piece of paper taped on) with a name or drawing to identify the owner.

When the seeds have grown a little, they can be replanted outside or into a larger pot.

Tip
Wait until the pots have been taken home to water them as if they are dropped the soil makes less mess if it is dry.

Try this idea!
Hold a competition. First set a date. Whoever has the tallest sunflower by then is the winner.

Daffodils ●●

What you will need
* Thick paper
* Photocopiable daffodil template (page 146)
* Thick card (cereal box card will do)
* Egg box

What to do
Cut a daffodil from the thick paper and colour it yellow or orange. Cut one segment from an egg box and colour it yellow, inside and out. Glue the bottom of the egg box segment to the centre of the flower. Make a stalk from thick card. Glue the flower to the top of the stalk. Cut two long thin leaves from the thick paper, colour them green and attach them to the bottom of the stalk.

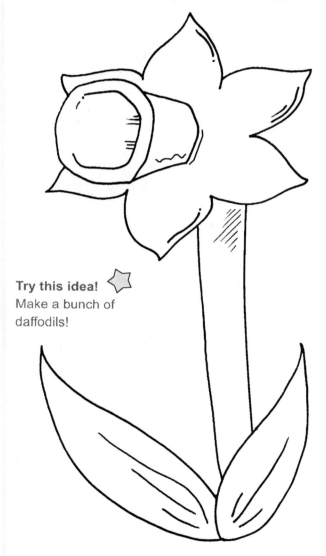

Try this idea!
Make a bunch of daffodils!

Painting activity
Potato printing. Cut potatoes in half and carve simple shapes into the cut surfaces. Put them out with saucers of paint and lots of paper.

Talk about
* Spring and the other seasons

* Bring in a bunch of daffodils for the children to look at and touch

* Sunflowers: explain how they can grow tall, have lots of seeds and are good to eat (and how the birds love them)

* Bring in some sunflower seeds for the children to taste

Stories
* *Jack and the Beanstalk*
  There are hundreds of versions of this favourite fairy tale.

* *Sunshine, Showers and Four O'clock Flowers* by Pauline Stewart and Nick Maland (Bodley Head Children's Books)

Songs and rhymes

We went for a ride on the bus today

Sit on the floor with straight legs, the children sitting on top or separately. The song starts and the verses go round the group with each child (at their bus stop) saying their name if they want to.

We went for a ride on the bus today
And who do you think we saw?
'Bertie'
And on he got and off we went,
Bumpety, bumpety, bumpety, bump
And who do you think we saw?
'Amy'
And on she got and off we went,
Bumpety, bumpety, bumpety, bump
And who do you think we saw?
'Lydia and Victoria'
And on they got…
Bumpety, bumpety, bumpety,
Bumpety, bumpety, bumpety, bump.
   last line getting quieter and quieter

Did you ever see a lassie

Keep everyone in position, ready for the adults to jiggle the children up and down. (If there are not enough adults, the children can jiggle themselves.) Say, 'Now we are all on the bus we are going on a journey along some very windy roads, so put on your seat belts and hold on tight!' Adults put their arms round the children's waists.

Did you ever see a lassie, a lassie, a lassie?
Did you ever see a lassie go this way and that?
> *start to rock from side to side, leaning over as far as you can.*
Go this way and that way
And this way and that way.
Did you ever see a lassie go this way and that?

Did you ever see a laddie, a laddie, a laddie?…

Daffy-down-dilly

A very easy rhyme that is really a riddle.

Daffy-down-dilly is new come to town,
With a yellow petticoat, and a green gown.

Other suggestions

✳ Baa baa black sheep

✳ Little Bo Peep

✳ If you're happy and you know it (see page 73)

✳ The bare necessities
This is marvellous for dancing about to with scarves.

Finish with the Good-bye song on page 8.

Creative Activities for the Early Years

Craft activities

Horse and cart

What you will need
* A4 paper
* Photocopiable horse and cart template (page 147)
* Hay
* Green tissue paper (optional)

What to do
Before the session, cut out the horse and cart and some wheel shapes, and put them out with the hay for the children to make their own picture.

Load the cart with hay and the horse can pull it. Colour the horse and draw on some eyes and a mouth. Scrunch up green tissue for grass and finally add a background.

What to do
Before the session, place both pieces of paper 'landscape view' and in one piece cut a stable door (top and bottom halves can open separately), leaving the 'hinged' side attached. Fold it open. Cut a small window at about the same level as the top part of the door, again leaving one side attached and fold that open too. Place the second piece of paper under the first and carefully tape them together across the top edge only.

Decorate the outside of the stable: colour the door, add some horseshoes on the wall, perhaps some ivy. Colour in the horse and add eyes and a mouth. Lift the top sheet of paper up and glue some hay on the floor of the stable, particularly in the doorway.

Tip
Don't use too much hay or the stable will be very lumpy.

Glue the horse in place, checking to make sure he can be seen through the door and window. Pull the top sheet back down and glue to the bottom sheet, leaving the door and window free to open and close.

Horse in a stable ●●

What you will need
* 2 sheets A4 paper
* Photocopiable horse shape (page 147)
* Hay

Lucky horseshoe

What you will need
* Card (cereal box card is ideal)
* Tin foil or silver paper
* Ribbon or string

What to do
Cut a life-size horseshoe shape from the card. Cover it with tin foil, caught at the back with tape. Use black felt pen (or similar) to mark the nail holes around the horseshoe. Attach some ribbon to the top and hang up your lucky horseshoe.

Tip
Horseshoes are usually hung with the ends pointing upwards, to keep the luck from falling out!

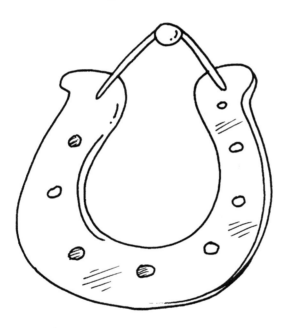

Painting activity

Put out horse and other animal stencils, sponges or rollers, saucers of paint, and lots of paper.

Tip
Packs of plastic animal stencils can be bought from shops and pre-school catalogues. They are reasonably priced and can last for ever!

Talk about
* Who has seen a horse? Has anyone stroked a horse or even had a ride on one?

* What do horses like to eat?

* What are baby horses called?

Stories
* *Oh Dear!* a lift-the-flap book by Rod Campbell. (Macmillan Children's Books)

* *Brown Bear, Brown Bear, What Do You See?* by Bill Martin and Eric Carle (Puffin Books)

* *Eat Up Piglittle* by Sally Grindley and Andy Ellis (Little Orchard Books)

Songs and rhymes

Horsey, horsey

Young children love to jog up and down on an adult's knee for this one. Older children can do the actions.

Horsey, horsey, don't you stop,
Just let your feet go clippety clop;
Your tail goes swish
And the wheels go round,
Giddy-up we're homeward bound.

© Barbara Melling
www.brilliantpublications.co.uk

Ride a cock horse

This well-known rhyme is fun if the adults sit on the floor and the children sit on their pulled-up knees, jiggling up and down.

Ride a cock-horse to Banbury Cross,
To see a fine lady upon a white horse.
With rings on her fingers and bells on her toes
    tickle the children's fingers and toes
She shall have music wherever she goes.

Trot, trot, trot

This favourite rhyme can be chanted or sung. The tune can be found on many tapes and CDs.

Trot, trot, trot, go and never stop.
Trudge along my little pony,
Where it's rough and where it's stony.
Go and never stop,
Trot, trot, trot, trot, trot.

Shoe a little horse

Shoe a little horse,
Shoe a little mare,
But let the little colt go bare, bare, bare.

This well-known rhyme is good for playing instruments to – shakers, bells, rattles and so on.

Other suggestions

* Yankee Doodle came to town

* This is the way the ladies ride

* Little green frog song (see page 12)

* Old MacDonald (see page 13)
  Can be found on many recordings.

* Widdicombe fair
  A good marching song.

Finish with the Good-bye song on page 8.

Craft activities

Chick collage

What you will need
* Photocopiable egg and chick template (page 148)
* Paper
* Straw (optional)

What to do
Cut out and colour some chick and egg shapes. Cut the eggs in half in a zigzag line. Glue the chicks to a piece of paper and stick the egg halves on either side of each chick. Older children might attempt to match the chicks to an appropriately sized egg. Finish the chicks by making a beak from a small diamond of orange paper. Fold it in half, glue the bottom half to the centre of the chick and leave the top half loose. Add eyes and feet. Draw straw (or use the real thing) on the ground.

Try this idea!
Cut out all the pieces for the eggs, chicks and beaks in advance and put them out with straw and crayons so that everyone can make their own collage unaided. Don't worry if the shapes get torn or stuck together or maybe don't look like the original – we all do things differently!

Easter bonnets

What you will need
* Thin coloured card
* Coloured tissue paper
* Crêpe paper
* Ribbon (optional)
* Streamers, beads, shiny paper, cotton wool

What to do
Cut a circle from the card about 26cm across and cut a line from the edge to the centre.

Tip
Use a dinner plate to draw round for the circle.

Overlap the straight edges by about 10cm (at the outer edge) and tape them together to make a wide conical hat. Decorate the bonnet with scrunched-up tissue paper, cotton wool, coloured and shiny paper, beads – anything you have that will make it beautiful. Attach a ribbon or strip of crêpe paper on each side to tie under the chin.

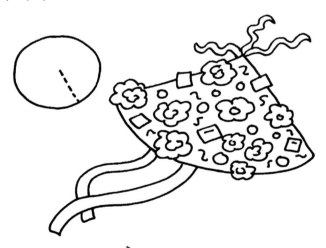

Try this idea!
Some boys may prefer a plainer bonnet. Choose a darker colour card and attach lots of streamers to the top peak. Add a fringe of tissue or streamers to the outside edge.

Chocolate nests ○ ○ ○

What you will need
* Cooking chocolate
* Shredded wheat breakfast cereal
* Small candied Easter eggs
* Large bowl
* Cake cases

What to do
Half fill a large bowl with hot water and put a smaller bowl containing the broken chocolate into it until the chocolate melts. Remove the small bowl from the water. Loosely crumble the shredded wheat, add it to the chocolate and mix well. The wheat will be the sticks of the nest and the chocolate the mud, so use lots of sticks and less mud. Put some nest mix into a cake case and slightly hollow out the centre. Place three or four candied Easter eggs inside and leave to set. Name the nests.

Tip
If the mixture begins to set hard before you are ready, pop the bowl back into hot water for a few minutes.

Tip
Make sure you have plenty of eggs – they tend to disappear and it would never do to run out!

Try this idea!
Allow the children to help make up the mixture as well as making their own nests.

Painting activity
Cut large paper egg shapes and let the children paint colourful Easter eggs.

Talk about
* How birds make their nests and what they use them for

* Hens lay eggs that we can eat and chicks hatch from eggs

* Chocolate eggs: who likes them, who does not

Stories
* *Happy Easter Davy!* by Brigitte Weninger and Eve Tharlet (North-South Books)

* *Oh Dear!* a lift-the-flap book by Rod Campbell (Macmillan Children's Books)

* *Friends* by Kim Lewis (Walker Books)

Songs and rhymes

Higgledy Piggledy, my black hen

A well-known rhyme, excellent for chanting while playing instruments.

Higgledy Piggledy, my black hen,
She lays eggs for gentlemen.
Sometimes nine and sometimes ten,
Higgledy Piggledy, my black hen.

Chook, chook, chook, chook, chook

Another fun rhyme for chanting, singing or playing instruments along to.

Chook, chook, chook, chook, chook,
Good morning, Mrs Hen.
How many chickens have you got?
Madam, I've got ten:
Four of them are yellow,
And four of them are brown,
And two of them are speckled red,
The nicest in the town.

Cock-a-doodle doo!

Cock-a-doodle doo!
My dame has lost her shoe;
My master's lost his fiddling stick,
And I don't know what to do.

Cock-a-doodle doo!
What is my dame to do?
'Till master finds his fiddling stick,
She'll dance without her shoe.

Cock-a-doodle doo!
My dame has found her shoe,
And master's found his fiddling stick,
Sing doodle doodle doo!

Cock-a-doodle doo!
My dame will dance with you,
While master fiddles his fiddling stick,
For dame and doodle doo.

Other suggestions

* Humpty Dumpty (see page 49)

* Sing a song of sixpence

* Hot cross buns

* Five brown eggs
  This counting song is good for marching with instruments.

* Chick, chick, chick, chick, chicken
  Fun to dance to.

* Hey little hen
  A lovely song for dancing to with scarves.

Finish with the Good-bye song on page 8.

Creative Activities for the Early Years

Garden insects

Craft activities

Ladybirds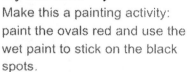

What you will need
* Thick A4 paper or larger
* Black paper

What to do
Before the session, cut out large ovals from the A4 paper and circles about 4cm across from the black paper. Colour the ovals red. Stick on some black spots. Add some eyes, a mouth and six simple legs.

Try this idea!
Make this a painting activity: paint the ovals red and use the wet paint to stick on the black spots.

Caterpillars ⚫⚫

What you will need
* Coloured felt
* Lolly sticks or straws
* Feathers, fabric scraps, wool, etc

What to do
Cut a caterpillar shape from the felt, about 20cm long and 4cm wide and with wavy edges. Decorate both sides with pieces of feather, fabric or wool and add eyes and mouth. Glue a lolly stick or straw to each end of the caterpillar and make him wiggle about!

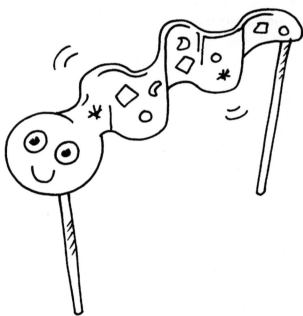

Bees ⚪⚪⚫

What you will need
* Cardboard tubes - small
* Bubble wrap
* String
* Pipe cleaners or straws
* Thin card

What to do
Paint (or crayon) black and yellow stripes round a cardboard tube and leave to dry.

Tip
Paint yellow first
and leave to dry,
then paint black.

Cut two circles from the thin card to fit the ends of the cardboard tube. Colour them yellow and draw a face on one circle. Cut two wings (attached, as in the drawing) from the bubble wrap. When the tube is completely dry make a small hole with a pencil point in the centre and push the middle of the pair of wings into it, leaving the wings sticking up. The wings should stay in place if the hole is small enough or else add a touch of glue.

Attach the face to one end of the tube with sticky tape or glue and add the other circle to the back end. For the antennae bend the ends of a pipe cleaner or straw to make little lumps, then bend it in half and secure the middle to the top of the head. Tape a piece of string to the centre of the bee for hanging.

Try this idea!
Make a swarm of bees and hang them together for an amusing effect!

Painting activity

Butterflies: fold large sheets of paper (at least A3 size) in half and using as much of the paper as possible cut half a butterfly shape against the fold. Unfold the paper and lay it flat again. Using lots of bright colours paint one or both wings of the butterfly. Carefully fold the paper again, pressing down to spread the paint onto both sides. Open it up and there you have your beautiful butterfly!

Try this idea!
For a colourful display, make lots of smaller butterflies. Attach thin string or cotton to the unpainted side, then suspend them, painted side down, in flight overhead.

Talk about

✳ How bees collect pollen from flowers and make honey from it. Have some honey for everyone to taste

✳ How caterpillars turn into butterflies

Stories

✳ *The Very Hungry Caterpillar* by Eric Carle (Hamish Hamilton Children's Books)

✳ *If at First You Do Not See* by Ruth Brown (Henry Holt and Company)

Songs and rhymes

Under a stone

Under a stone where the earth is warm,
I found a wiggly, wiggly worm,
'Good morning' said I, 'How are you today?'
But the wiggly worm just wiggled away.

Hold first finger of right hand (worm) under outstretched left hand (stone). Remove 'stone' and talk to wiggling 'worm'. For last line, 'worm' wiggles away to tickle nearest child.

There's a tiny caterpillar

Sung to the tune of 'She'll be coming round the mountain'.

There's a tiny caterpillar on a leaf, wiggle, wiggle,
There's a tiny caterpillar on a leaf, wiggle, wiggle,
There's a tiny caterpillar, tiny caterpillar,
There's a tiny caterpillar on a leaf, wiggle, wiggle.
> *wiggle finger of one hand on open 'leaf' of the other*

He will eat the leaves around him 'til he's full,
    munch, munch…
> *open and shut fingers and thumbs*

A cocoon is what he's spinning for his home, spin,
    spin…
> *'spin' hands round each other*

Then he'll be a butterfly and flap away, flap, flap…
> *link thumbs and flap both hands, or flap arms*

So the tiny caterpillar went like this:
Wiggle, wiggle, munch, munch, spin, spin, flap,
    flap…
> *try to do all the actions (good luck!)*

Ladybird, ladybird

This well-known rhyme can be chanted to an accompaniment of instruments.

Ladybird, ladybird, fly away home,
Your house is on fire, your children all gone,
All except one and that's little Ann
And she crept under the warming pan.

Round and round the garden

Round and round the garden like a teddy bear,
One step, two steps, tickle you under there.

Child holds hand out flat, palm up, and adult 'walks' two fingers round the 'garden' (the palm) then takes one step, two steps, up child's arm and tickles under arm.

Other suggestions

✳ Mary, Mary, quite contrary

✳ I had a little nut tree

✳ Here we go round the mulberry bush

✳ Ring-a-ring o' roses

Finish with Good-bye song on page 8.

Craft activities

Castle collage

What you will need

* Large piece of paper
* Pre-cut shapes

What to do

Before the session, cut out lots of castle shapes, different sized rectangles and triangles. Don't forget to cut some with 'battlements'. Let the children choose which shapes they want and encourage them to stick them on the paper to create their own castle. Add some details to the building such as a door, windows, flags and brickwork. Add some details to the surroundings such as a pathway, some trees and bushes and some clouds.

> **Tip** ⭐
> Don't worry if the castles look different from the one you have made as everyone has their own ideas.

Crowns ⚫⚫

What you will need

* Thin card (at least 55cm in length)
* Cotton wool
* Coloured and shiny paper
* Glittery bits and pieces to decorate

What to do

Cut a length of card at least 12cm wide and long enough to fit around the child's head. Cut a zigzag line along one edge to a depth of about 5cm.

> **Tip** ⭐
> Use a strip of card at least 24 cm wide and cut a zigzag line down the centre. This will give you two crowns shapes and no card to waste.

Glue a thin strip of cotton wool along the straight edge and with a black felt pen (or similar) mark dots on it at about 3cm intervals. Decorate the rest of the crown with coloured and shiny paper and glittery bits and pieces.

> **Tip** ⭐
> Scrunched-up toffee wrappers make excellent jewels.

When the crown is finished and the glue is dry, measure it round the child's head and join the ends together.

> **Tip**
> If you use staples, face them outwards to avoid catching any hair.

© Barbara Melling
www.brilliantpublications.co.uk

Pasta jewellery ◉ ◉

What you will need
* Dried 'penne' pasta (macaroni can be used, but it is not as good)
* String
* Thin card circle about 6cm across
* Gold or silver paper
* Glitter (optional)

What to do
Colour the pasta shapes using paint or pens, or glue on coloured paper or glitter. This can be lovely and messy so be prepared! Decorate the card circle with gold paper, jewels and glitter and make a small hole in the top. Thread a piece of string through and make a small loop.

When the pasta is dry, thread it onto the string until you have enough for a long necklace (or chain of office!) that will comfortably fit over the head. Thread the loop of the card circle onto the string and tie the ends together.

Wear the chain with the golden medallion hanging in the front. Adorned with this and the crown, the wearer becomes quite regal!

Painting activity

Cut some battlements along the top edge of the paper (you can easily do five or six at a time) and allow the children to paint their own castles.

Talk about
* The queen: what she wears, where she lives

* Has anyone visited a castle before or seen a picture of one?

* How do the children feel when they wear their crowns and chains?

Stories
* *Stella, Queen of the Snow* by Marie-Louise Gay (Groundwood Books)

* *Princesses are not Quitters*! by Kate Lum (Bloomsbury Children's Books)

* *The Witch's Children and the Queen* by Ursula Jones and Russell Ayto (Orchard Books)

Songs and rhymes

The grand old Duke of York

Not quite royalty, but never mind! A wonderful song for marching around the room to while playing instruments.

The grand old Duke of York,
He had ten thousand men,
He marched them up to the top of the hill
And he marched them down again.
And when they were up, they were up,
And when they were down, they were down,
And when they were only halfway up,
They were neither up nor down.

Stretch up high for the 'up's and go down low for the 'down's.

Royal rock-a-bye baby

A 'royal' version of this well-known lullaby.

Rock-a-bye baby, thy cradle is green,
Father's a nobleman, mother's a queen;
And Betty's a lady, and wears a gold ring;
And Johnny's a drummer, and drums for the king.

Other suggestions

✳ The queen of hearts

✳ The poor king found a goldfish in his bath

✳ Sing a song of sixpence

✳ Old King Cole

✳ I had a little nut tree

✳ Humpty Dumpty (see page 49)

✳ I wanna be like you
This song from the Jungle Book *is good for joining in with instruments or dancing to.*

Finish with the Good-bye song on page 8.

Creative Activities for the Early Years

Birds

Craft activities

Bird's nest

What you will need
* Paper (at least A4 size)
* Paper shapes (can be cut out in advance)
* Straw

What to do

Place your paper 'landscape' view. From a second piece of paper cut out a simple nest shape (like a very fat curved sausage), big enough to fill the middle of your paper, and glue it on. Cut three simple baby bird head shapes (slightly different sizes if possible). For the beaks, cut three small diamond shapes from yellow or orange paper, fold them in half and glue the lower half in place, leaving the top half free. Add some big eyes and any other detail you may want. Glue the birds in the nest. Next, using lots of glue, stick some straw onto the nest, covering it if possible. Add further details such as branches, leaves and sky.

Flying birds

What you will need
* Thin card
* Photocopiable bird template (page 149)
* Coloured tissue paper
* Feathers
* String

What to do

Cut out the bird shape from thin card and cut a 4cm horizontal slit in the centre 1cm from the top. Decorate the bird on both sides with feathers and other bits and pieces, but leave the slit free. Add eyes and a beak.

Take a piece of coloured tissue paper approximately 20cm square and fold it into a fan. While it is still folded, push one end through the slit in the bird and pull it through until there is an equal length on both sides. Open out the tissue to make wings (the folds should keep the wings in place but secure with a little tape if not).

Attach a piece of string to the top centre of the bird, hang him up and watch him fly around.

Try this idea!
Make a colourful flock of birds to fly across the room!

Bird puppet

What you will need
* 2 paper plates
* String
* Crêpe or tissue paper, feathers, wool, etc.
* Butterfly clips (paper fasteners)

What to do
Draw two big eyes and a beak on one of the plates. Divide the second plate into two wing shapes and two smaller feet shapes (see drawing), and cut them out. Colour and decorate the face, wings and feet.

Tip ☆

Try not to use too much 'lumpy' material to decorate the face, otherwise the wings won't move.

Using the butterfly clips attach a wings either side of the face. Fasten the butterfly clips loosely so that the wings move freely. For the legs, thread two pieces of string, at least 20cm long, through the bottom of the face and knot them. Thread the other ends of the string through the middle of the feet and knot them again. Attach another piece of string to the top of the bird puppet to hold it by.

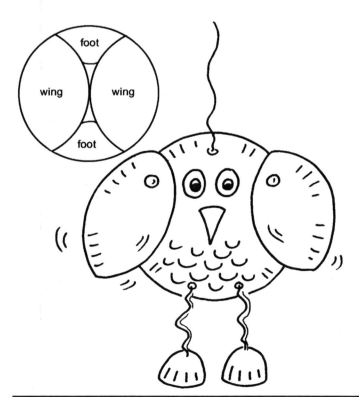

Painting activity
Put out lots of paints, brushes and paper and allow the children to paint what they want.

Talk about
* Different birds: can the children name any (robin, sparrow, blackbird, seagull...)?

* Has anyone seen a bird's nest? Someone may have an old one they could show the others

* What do birds like to eat? Does anyone put crumbs out for them?

Stories
* *Owl Babies* by Martin Waddell (Walker Books)

* *The Gossipy Parrot* by Shen Roddie (Bloomsbury)

* *Come On Baby Duck!* by Nick Ward (LittleTiger Press)

Songs and rhymes

Two little dickey birds
Use one finger on each hand for the simple actions of this rhyme: make them fly away behind your back, then bring them back again.

Two little dickey birds sitting on a wall,
One named Peter, one named Paul.
Fly away Peter, fly away Paul.
Come back Peter, come back Paul.

Once I saw a little bird

This rhyme is chanted and the actions are best done standing up.

Once I saw a little bird
Going hop, hop, hop;
   hop about
So I cried, 'Little bird
Will you stop, stop, stop?'
   hands up to mouth and shout
And was going to the window
To say, 'How do you do?'
   shake hands with other people
But he shook his little tail
And away he flew.
   wiggle bottom and flap arms

I had two pigeons

A simple rhyme for chanting and playing instruments to.

I had two pigeons bright and gay,
They flew from me the other day;
What was the reason they did go?
I cannot tell, for I do not know.

Other suggestions

* Under a stone (see page 85)

* Sing a song of sixpence

* Cock-a-doodle doo! (see page 82)

* Seagull, seagull, sit on the shore
  (see page 118)

* Goosey goosey gander

Finish with the Good-bye song on page 8.

Craft activities

Clothes cupboard ⊙

What you will need
* Thick paper (A4 size sheets)
* Pictures of clothes cut out of magazines and catalogues
* Butterfly clips (paper fasteners) – optional

What to do
Place the paper 'landscape' view and fold both sides in to meet in the middle. These two flaps are the cupboard doors. Decorate the outside of the cupboard and add some door knobs (either draw them or fix some butterfly clips through). Open the doors. Fill the cupboard by gluing in pictures of clothes. You could add some shelves by drawing in some lines if you want.

What to do
Place the paper 'landscape' view. Cut out two thin strips of paper about 14cm long for clothes posts. Stick them on the paper about 20cm apart. Glue a length of string from one post to the other for the clothes-line.

Cut out simple clothing shapes from pieces of fabric. Cut rectangles for towels and table-cloths. Choose different colours, textures and patterns. Glue them on the line and draw some pegs where they touch. Fill in the background details.

Try this idea! ✩
For a simple collage the children can make by themselves, cut out a selection of clothing shapes and allow the children to choose the pieces they like.

Clothes-line ⊙ ⊙

What you will need
* Thin string
* A4 paper
* Scraps of different fabric

Washing machine ⊙ ⊙ ⊙

What you will need
* Thin card (approx. 15 x 21cm or A5)
* Clear plastic or polythene (from a plastic bag or food wrap)
* Blu-tak – optional

What to do

Cut a 10cm circle from thin card. Draw a 7cm circle in the centre of the card and cut out the middle, leaving a ring. This can be pre-cut.

Tip
Draw round a large reel of sticky tape, inside and outside.

Place the ring (the window) in the centre of the rectangular card (the machine) and draw around the inside of the middle hole. Cut an 8cm circle of clear plastic and stick it across the hole in the card. This is the door, with it's window (leave out the window if you wish). Turn the door over (to hide the join) and with a neat piece of tape attach it to the centre of the machine over the previously drawn circle, so that it opens to the left or right.

Colour and add details to the machine eg. knobs and dials. Open the door and draw some small clothes inside the circle, maybe a few socks and some pants. Use another neat piece of tape (or Blu-tak) to fasten the door shut. It is easy to peel back the tape to open the door and have a peep at the clothes inside.

Try this idea!
If you don't want to draw clothes, cut out pictures from catalogues and stick them on!

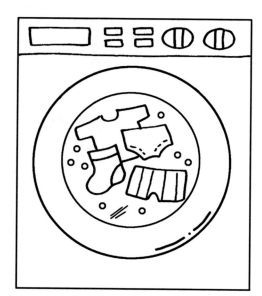

Painting activity

Cut simple clothes shapes from large sheets of paper, one from each piece. Use sponges or brushes and lots of bright colours to paint the clothing.

Try this idea!
Use a line of string and pegs to dry the pictures and you will have a lovely colourful clothes-line as the paintings dry.

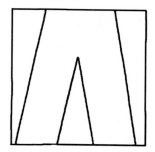

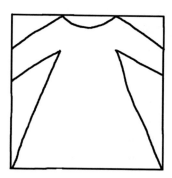

Talk about

* Has everyone seen a washing machine? What do they do?

* Why do lots of people hang their washing outside? When is it a good time to hang wet clothes out to dry? When would it be a bad idea?

* Clothes and their uses (warmth, protection from the sun, and so on). Favourite clothes: comfortable clothes, bright clothes, clothes for favourite pastimes (for example, swimming costumes, wellington boots)

Stories

* *Here's Buster – But Where's Teddy?* a lift-the-flap book by Rod Campbell (Campbell Books)

* *There's a Monster in my House* a lift-the-flap book by Jenny Tyler and Philip Hawthorn (Usborne Books)

* *Hurry Up, Jessie!* by Harriet Ziefert and Mavis Smith (Harper Collins Children's Books)

Songs and rhymes

This is the way we wash our clothes

An easy action song, sung to the tune of 'Here we go round the mulberry bush.'

This is the way we wash our clothes,
Rub-a-dub-dub, rub-a-dub-dub;
See them getting clean and white,
Rub-a-dub, rub-a-dub-dub!

This is the way we hang them out,
Flippity-flap, flippity-flap;
See them blowing in the wind,
Flippity-flippity-flap!

This is the way we iron them,
Smooth as can be, smooth as can be;
Soon our wash-day will be done,
And nice clean clothes for you and me.

I went to visit a friend one day

Either chant this rhyme, or make up a simple tune to sing it to.

I went to visit a friend one day,
She only lived across the way;
She said she couldn't come out to play
Because it was her washing day.

…Because it was her drying day.

…Because it was her ironing day.

Our washing machine

This funny rhyme is perfect for using different instruments to make the noises.

Our washing machine went wisharty whir, wisharty
   whir.
One day it went wisharty click, wisharty click,
Click, whir, click, whir, click, whir, click.
Call the repair man, FIX IT QUICK!

Other suggestions

* Three little kittens

* Diddle diddle dumpling, my son John

* Soldier, soldier, won't you marry me?

* Itsy bitsy teeny weeny yellow polka dot bikini
  Play instruments along to this one.

* Simple Simon says
  Great for dancing with scarves or just do the actions.

Finish with the Good-bye song on page 8.

© Barbara Melling
www.brilliantpublications.co.uk

Clocks

Craft activities

Clock

What you will need
* Large paper plate
* Butterfly clip (paper fasteners)
* Thin card

What to do
Colour the plate with pens or paint.

Cut two hands from thin card, a big hand and a little hand, and decorate them. Make twelve evenly spaced marks on the clock face and draw in the numbers. Attach the two hands to the centre of the clock face with a loose butterfly clip.

Try this idea!
Try putting some suitable pictures (for example, a sandwich at 1, a bed at 7) by the numbers or alternatively, a flower behind each number.

Cuckoo clock ○○○

What you will need
* Thin card in two contrasting colours (pre-cut shapes)
* Straws or pipe cleaners
* Butterfly clip (paper fastener)

What to do
You could cut out all the shapes before the session. Cut a rectangle approximately A5 size from thin card for the house. Use coloured card, or colour the card yourself. Cut a triangle approximately 18 x 18 x 21cm in a contrasting colour to make the roof. Find the centre of the long edge and make a cut 4cm long. Fold back the edges from the cut.

Stick the long edge of the roof onto the shorter edge of the rectangle, overlapping it by about 4cm. Make a loop of string and tape it to the top of the roof for hanging.

Cut a circle about 10cm across and draw the numbers 1–12 for the clock face. Stick the clock onto the centre of the house and decorate. Cut two hands and attach them with a butterfly clip to the centre of the clock face, pushing all the way through.

Tip ☆
Leave the butterfly clip a little loose so that the clock hands will move.

Cut out a small cuckoo (a simple cloud shape) about 4cm high and colour him. Cut a tiny diamond shape for the beak, fold it in half and glue half to the cuckoo so the top half sticks out. Add some eyes. Fold an 8 x 2cm strip of card into a fan shape. Tape one end to the cuckoo and attach the other to the opening you folded back in the roof.

Creative Activities for the Early Years

To make the pendulums, cut two oval shapes (the roof off-cuts are good for this as the colour will match) and tape or staple them to the ends of two straws. Make one straw a little shorter than the other. Attach both straws to the back of the house so they hang down underneath the clock. Set the hands to the time you want and hang your cuckoo clock up on the wall.

Hickory dickory

dock

What you will need
* Thin card (A4) (colour 1)
* Thin card square approx 16 x 16cm (colour 2)
* Thin card strips (colour 3)
* Small piece of fur fabric
* Felt
* Thin string
* Butterfly clip

What to do
Take the square of card (colour 2) and draw a large circle onto it (draw around a saucer), draw in the numbers 1–12 for the clock face. Cut two clock hands and pendulum (a strip 20 x 2cm) from thin card (colour 3) and, using a butterfly clip, attach the hands to the front of the clock face and the pendulum behind.

Cut a circle (approx 5cm) from thin card (use silver or gold if you have it) and attach it to the bottom of the pendulum. Turn the clock face over and glue down both sides of the square, turn it back over and, with the pendulum hanging down, attach it to the top half of the A4 thin card (colour 1) portrait view.

Tip
Make sure the lower edge is free from glue to allow the pendulum to move freely.

Thread a length of thin string approx. 50cm through the top and bottom of the A4 card about 4cm in from the right edge and about 4cm from the top and lower edges and tie it together on the front of the picture, making a loop.

Tip
Make sure the loop is fairly tight and not too saggy.

Cut a 7 x 7cm piece of fur fabric (use felt if you prefer) and folding it over, glue it onto itself over the knot with the string going through the length. This is the mouse. If you wish, trim the top into a pointed nose shape and add a tiny felt nose. Cut two small circles from felt and glue them on for ears. Set the clock hands to 1 o'clock and pull the loop of string at the back of the picture up and down to make the mouse run up and down the clock!

Creative Activities for the Early Years

Painting activity

Put out paints, brushes and paper and allow the children to paint what they like.

Talk about

* Clocks: what do they do?

* Different times of the day: dinner time, bedtime, story time, and so on. What are the children's favourite times (time to go shopping, to visit Grandma, to go to nursery)?

* What else can tell us the time? The sun coming up or going down, a cock crowing, the school bell, our tummies rumbling!

Stories

* *Fidget and Quilly, Are You Ready?* a lift-the-flap book by Mike Haines and David Melling (Hodder Children's Books)

* *Bath Water's Hot* by Shirley Hughes (Walker Books)

* *Good Morning Little Fox* by Marilyn Janovitz (North-South Books)

Songs and rhymes

Mr Moon, you're up too soon

This jolly song can be sung to the tune of 'Jack and Jill.' Jump up and raise arms to sky on first two lines. Lie down, put arms over head and sleep on the next three.

Mr Moon, you're up too soon,
The sun's still in the sky;
Go back to bed
And cover your head,
You must wait till the day's gone by.

Cobbler, cobbler

See page 98 for music.

Cobbler, cobbler, mend my shoe,
   hammer with fists on knees
Get it done by half past two.
Stitch it up and stitch it down
   raise arms and lower arms
Then I'll give you half-a-crown.
   hammer with fists again

The cock crows in the morn

Perfect for chanting while playing on instruments.

The cock crows in the morn
To tell us to rise,
And he that lies late
Will never be wise;
For early to bed
And early to rise
Is the way to be healthy
And wealthy and wise!

Slowly, slowly, very slowly

The actions to this little rhyme can be mimed with hands, but it's more fun walking slowly and running fast!

Slowly, slowly, very slowly
Creeps the garden snail.
Slowly, slowly, very slowly
Up the wooden rail.

Quickly, quickly, very quickly
Runs the little mouse.
Quickly, quickly, very quickly
Round about the house.

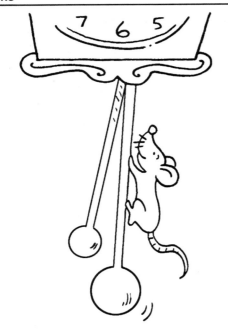

Other suggestions

＊ Hickory dickory dock (see page 67)

＊ Cock-a-doodle doo! (see page 82)

＊ Polly put the kettle on (see page 73)

＊ I went to school this morning
This song has plenty of 'large' actions to accompany it.

＊ She'll be coming round the mountain

Finish with the Good-bye song on page 8.

Cobbler, cobbler

Creative Activities for the Early Years

Magic

Craft activities

Wizard's beard ○

What you will need
* Stiff paper
* Cotton wool
* Thin string or elastic

What to do
Cut a long triangle from stiff paper, the shortest side wide enough to fit across the face (about 10cm for a child, 15cm for an adult) and the point as long as you want your beard. Attach two loops of string or elastic to the corners of the short side to fit round your ears. Glue on cotton wool to make a lovely long white beard.

Wizard's hat ○○

What you will need
* Large sheet of coloured paper
* White or grey wool or cotton wool
* Stars and moon to decorate
* Thin string or elastic

What to do
Curl a large sheet of coloured paper into a cone big enough for the open end to fit the head. Join the overlapping edges together with tape or staples and trim the lower edge straight. Decorate the hat with lots of stars and crescent moons. You may want to attach some thin string or elastic to the hat to go under your chin.

For wizard's hair, cut lengths of white or grey wool and stick the ends onto a piece of sticky tape. Stick the tape to the inside of the rim so the hair hangs down from the hat. Alternatively, staple a thick strip of cotton wool around the inside of the rim of the hat so that most of it hangs below the rim.

Put on the beard first and then the hat, letting the hair hang down around the face and, hey presto, a wizard!

Magic trick ◉ ◯

What you will need
* ✳ Black A4 paper
* ✳ White paper
* ✳ Glitter

What to do
Place a piece of black paper 'landscape' view and fold it in half from left to right (it's now 'portrait' view). Cut off a 3cm strip from across the top and keep it for the wand. Cut off a 3cm strip from both sides stopping 3cm from the top. This leaves the shape of an upturned top hat. Staple or tape round the sides and across the bottom, leaving the top open. Decorate the top hat with glitter or shiny stars.

Draw and cut out a simple sitting rabbit about 12cm tall (draw two circles, like a snowman, with two long ears on top). Add eyes, nose and whiskers. Take the strip of black paper kept for the wand (keeping it doubled for strength) and glue a piece of white paper to one end. Glue the other end of the wand to the back of the rabbit's head at an angle of about 45 degrees, so that the rabbit can slip into the top hat leaving only the end of the wand showing. To perform the trick, say the magic word 'abracadabra' and pull the wand from the top hat to reveal a white rabbit!

Painting activity
Cut out stencils of stars and moons from card (cereal boxes), or buy plastic stencils from shops or pre-school catalogues. Put the paint in saucers and use sponges to apply it.

Talk about
* ✳ Has anyone seen a magic show? Did they enjoy it?

* ✳ If the children could have three wishes, what would they choose?

* ✳ How many magic words can they think of? eg. 'Abracadabra', 'Hockus Pockus'. Can they make up their own magic words or phrases?

Stories
* ✳ *Room on the Broom* by Julia Donaldson and Axel Scheffler (Macmillan Children's Books)

* ✳ *The Witch's Children and the Queen* by Ursula Jones and Russell Ayto (Orchard Books)

* ✳ *Winnie's Magic Wand* by Valerie Thomas and Korky Paul (Oxford University Press)

Songs and rhymes

The wizard makes a spell
*A variation on 'The snowman's in his den'
on page 45.*

The wizard makes a spell,
The wizard makes a spell,
Abracadabra
The wizard makes a spell.

He conjures up a wife…

She conjures up a child…

(S)he conjures up a nurse…

(S)he conjures up a dog…

We all pat the dog…

Barbara Melling

Tommy Thumb

Bring your hands out from behind your back after 'Where are you?'

Tommy Thumb, Tommy Thumb,
Where are you?
Here I am, here I am,
How do you do?
   wiggle both thumbs and bow them together on the last line

Peter Pointer, Peter Pointer…
   repeat using index finger

Toby Tall, Toby Tall…
   use middle finger

Ruby Ring, Ruby Ring…
   use ring finger

Baby Small, Baby Small…
   use little finger

Fingers All, Fingers All…
   use all fingers

Heads, shoulders, knees and toes

*This well-known action song is great fun.
Check the children recognise all the body parts:
'Have we all got shoulders?' 'Has everyone
brought their nose with them today?' Traditionally,
a body part is left out each time, but this can
sometimes be difficult for very young children.
Instead, try doing it slowly at first, then a little
quicker and finally as fast as you can.*

Heads, shoulders, knees and toes, knees and
   toes,
Head, shoulders knees and toes, knees and toes,
and eyes and ears and mouth and nose,
Heads, shoulders, knees and toes, knees and
   toes.

Other suggestions

✳ Wind the bobbin up (see page 64)

✳ Puff the magic dragon and Lily the pink
   *Both these brilliant songs are found on many
   tapes and CDs.*

✳ Bibbidi-bobbidi boo
   From Disney's Cinderella.

✳ Supercalifragalisticexpialidocious
   From Disney's Mary Poppins.

Finish with the Good-bye song on page 8.

Craft activities

Height flower

What you will need

* Large sheet of thick coloured paper
* Strips of green paper 100 x 10cm
* Photo of a child (optional)

What to do

Before the session, cut a simple flower shape from the coloured paper (cut a circle approximately 30cm across and cut five big petal shapes into the edge). Cut a smaller (12cm) flower from a different coloured paper. Glue the photo, if you have one, to the centre of the smaller flower and write the name and age clearly around it or simply write the name and age in larger letters! Glue the small flower to the centre of the large flower, colour and decorate them.

Attach one end of the strip of green paper to the back of the flower for the stalk, making sure that the writing is the correct way up! Add more strips until the flower is as tall as the child, although young children will only need one. Trim from the bottom of the stalk until the height is right.

Attach the flowers to a wall, making sure the bottom of the stalks are at ground level. This makes a pretty height record of each child's height.

Try this idea!
Ask the children to bring in small photos of other people in their family. Attach them to leaves growing out from the stalk.

Self-portrait

If space or time is limited just make the face.

What you will need for the face

* Paper plates
* Lolly sticks or similar
* Wool, ribbon, shredded paper, material scraps, etc

What to do

Paint or colour the plate, remembering to add a little glue to the paint to make it stick. Add shredded paper or wool for hair, cut-out paper, buttons or milk bottle tops for eyes, paper or felt for lips. Add ribbons, scarves, bow ties. Tape the lolly stick to the bottom of the plate (the chin) for a handle.

What you will need for the whole body
* Roll of lining paper
* Wool, ribbon, shredded paper, material scraps, etc

What to do
Pull off a length of lining paper from the roll, a little taller than the child, and lay it on the floor, or hang it on a wall, making sure it touches the floor. Draw round the child as he lies on the paper or stands up against it (try to keep the crayon perpendicular to the paper to avoid 'stick' arms and legs). Paint or colour the figure and add details.

Hands and feet mobile ○○○

What you will need
* Thin card
* String
* Pea stick (or similar)

What to do
Draw round the hands and (bare) feet of the children and cut out the four shapes. For a bigger mobile do this twice to end up with eight shapes. Decorate the shapes and write the name, date or age of the child on each one. Tape strings to each shape and suspend them at different heights from the pea stick. Add a loop of string to the centre of the mobile to hang it up by.

Safety note ☆
Always be careful when using pea sticks with very small children. Do not leave the sticks loose on the table.

Try this idea! ☆
Encourage older children to pretend to be someone else: black hair instead of yellow, green trousers instead of a red dress, even a policeman or mermaid instead of a child!

Painting activity
If you are doing the large self-portraits there will be plenty of painting to keep everyone busy. If not put out brushes, paints and paper and allow 'free painting'.

Talk about

* How everyone is different and very special!

* Ask the children to list the best things about themselves: their curly/straight hair, strong legs for running fast, being small enough to hide well, or being good at hopping, for example

* What do the children like about being me? For example, 'I like having a big brother,' 'I like having a friend,' 'I like riding on Granddad's back'

Stories

* *Things I Like* by Anthony Browne (Walker Books)

* *My Friends and Me* by Pat Thomas (Hodder Wayland)

* *Once There Was A Hoodie* by Sam McBratney and Paul Hess (Hodder Children's)

Songs and rhymes

I went up one pair of stairs

Try this with the adult saying the lines 'I went…' and the children replying 'Just like me'.

I went up one pair of stairs,
Just like me.
I went up two pairs of stairs,
Just like me.
I went into a room,
Just like me.
I looked out of the window,
Just like me.
And there I saw a monkey,
Just like me.

Once a man walked on my toes

Starting at your toes, 'walk' your fingers up your body to your nose, then 'jump' them onto your head.

Once a man walked on my toes,
Along my legs, up to my nose;
'Go away,' I said, and so he jumped…
Right up onto my head!

If you should meet a giant

Stretch up high to be very tall and crouch down low to be very small.

If you should meet a giant,
Don't say 'You're very tall'!
Or he might take you in his hand…
And say, 'You're very SMALL'!

Other suggestions

* Heads, shoulders, knees and toes (see page 101)

* One finger, one thumb, keep moving.

* If you're happy and you know it (see page 73)

* We went for a ride on the bus today (see page 75)

* Criss cross apple sauce (see page 16)

* Here we go, Looby Loo (see page 35)

* Put your finger on your head (see page 49)

* John Brown stamped his feet
  This is a brilliant song for doing actions to.

* Simple Simon says

* Lil' Liza Jane
  Great fun to dance to.

Finish with the Good-bye song on page 8.

Craft activities

Tepee picture

What you will need
* A4 paper
* Black paper and paper in other colours
* Tissue paper

What to do
Before the session, cut a triangle about 22 x 22 x 18cm. Cut another (use black paper or colour it) about 8 x 8 x 6cm.

Place the A4 paper 'portrait view' and glue the large triangle in the middle as the tepee. Glue the small triangle in the centre at the bottom of the tepee, to make a door. Decorate the tepee by adding some 'sticks' to the top, stitching to show how it's made, and some patterns. Add grass, trees, clouds and birds to the picture. Draw a small pile of sticks outside the tepee, tear some red and yellow tissue pieces and glue them over the sticks for a fire.

Totem pole collage

What you will need
* Thick paper or thin card
* Materials to decorate

What to do
Before the session, cut three heads from thin card (cloud shapes), at least 15cm high.

Decorate the heads and add lots of features – eyes, mouths, beaks, hair, beards, noses, eyebrows, ears. The heads can be anything you want: animals, birds, monsters or people, happy or sad. Use lots of different materials such as tissue paper, shiny paper, foil, wool and fabrics. Arrange the heads one on top of another and tape them together at the back.

Try this idea!
To make an enormous group totem pole, use bigger head shapes and give one to each child. Assemble them all together against a wall or similar.

Feather headdress

What you will need

* Strip of thin card (80–100 x 5cm)
* Feathers (packets can be bought from craft shops or pre-school catalogues)

What to do

Decorate the strip of card, the head band, with paint or pens. Staple or tape some feathers (one at a time) to the middle part of the head band, so that they stand up. Put the band round the head, crossing the ends over each other at the back. Staple or tape together where they cross.

Budget buster!

To make your own feathers, cut a long oval shape from stiff paper and fold it in half lengthways. Make short snips down the open edge at a slight angle. Open the feather out and tape or staple a straw down the centre, leaving a short length free at the bottom.

Try this idea!
Use face paints to add some war paint!

Painting activity

Printing with sponge shapes is fun to do with this theme. Use lots of angular and linear designs together with bright colours to create patterns.

Tip
Make your own sponges from kitchen sponges cut into pieces.

Talk about

* Where native Americans live: in another country, a long way away, across the sea…

* How they used to live in tepees (which are like tents). Has anyone been inside a tent? Has anyone eaten a meal cooked outside on a fire?

* Can anyone make a funny face? Who can make the funniest, saddest, happiest face?

Stories

* *Lion's Precious Gift* by Barbara Bennett (Little Tiger Press)

* *Pedro the Brave* by Leo Broadley and Holly Swain (Scholastic Press)

Songs and rhymes

Ten little Indians

A version of 'Ten fat sausages.' Try it while wearing the feather headdress! Hold your hand, with palm straight, next to your face for 'How!' and tap your mouth with your fingers on 'Oooooo!'

Ten little Indians sitting on a wall
One went 'How!', and another went 'Oooooooo!'

Eight little Indians etc…

Six little Indians etc…

Creative Activities for the Early Years

John Brown met a little Indian

This counting song can be sung using fingers to count up to ten little Indians. It is also good as a 'bringing in' game: carry on until everyone has been brought into the group.

John Brown met a little Indian,
John Brown met a little Indian,
John Brown met a little Indian,
One little Indian boy.

Chorus
He met one little, two little, three little Indians,
Four little, five little, six little Indians,
Seven little, eight little, nine little Indians,
Ten little Indian boys.

John Brown met two little Indians…

The full version of the song has further verses:

Each little Indian had a bow and arrow /
little tepee / tomahawk / feather headdress / totem
pole…

Other suggestions

* Row, row, row the boat (see page 8)

* Jake the snake (see page 61)

* Clap your hands everyone together
  (see page 33)

* What shall I do with my two hands?
  (see page 30)

* Wind the bobbin (see page 64)

* She'll be coming round the mountain
  A good song for marching with instruments.

* Chip chop, chip chop, chipper chopper Joe
  This song is great for marching with instruments.

Finish with the Good bye song on page 8.

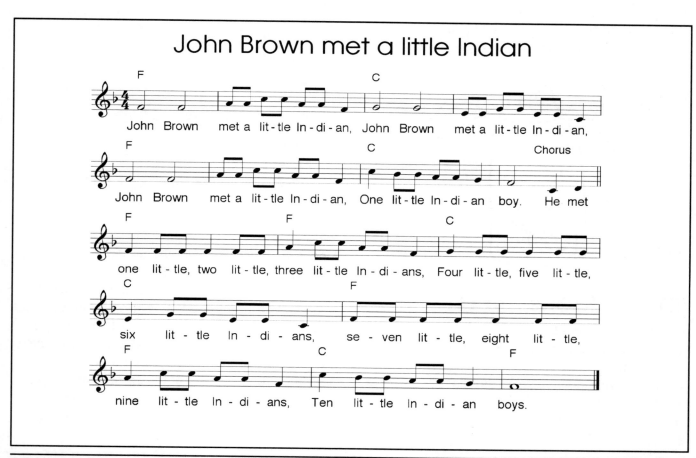

John Brown met a little Indian

Craft activities

Bottle shakers

What you will need
* Small plastic screw top bottles
* Rice, dried peas, lentils, small stones, etc
* Streamers, crêpe paper, ribbon, glitter (optional)

What to do
Make sure the bottles are completely dry. Put a handful of dried rice or other shakeable material into a bottle, add some glitter for sparkle if you wish, and screw the lid on tightly. Glue or tie some colourful streamers, crêpe paper strips or ribbon around the neck of the bottle and shake, shake, shake!

Tip
For the best sound, do not over fill the bottle. Up to a third full is about right.

Shaker tubes

What you will need
* Large cardboard tubes (kitchen roll or tin foil tubes)
* Rice, dried pulses, small stones, etc
* Streamers or crêpe paper
* Ribbons (optional)
* Tin foil or thin card circles (about 6–7 cm)

What to do
Paint or colour a tube and when dry tape a circle of tin foil or thin card over one end (snip the edges of the card to make it fit). Put a handful of dried pulses, rice or small stones into the tube and tape another foil or card circle over the other end. Decorate the ends by attaching streamers, strips of crêpe paper or ribbons. Shake the tubes or tip them up first one way and then the other.

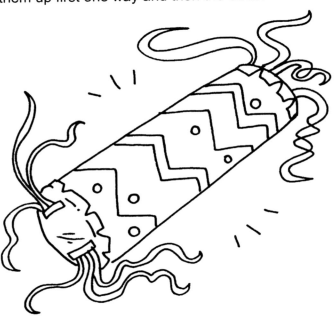

Tambourines

What you will need
* Paper plates
* Dried peas, lentils, small stones, etc
* Streamers or crêpe paper

What to do
Decorate, colour or paint the underside of two paper plates (leave to dry if painted). Put the plates together, coloured sides facing outwards and staple round the edge, leaving a gap of about 5cm. Cut some streamers from coloured crêpe paper. Put a handful of dried peas or similar into the gap left around the edge of the plates and, catching the streamers at the same time, staple the edges together to secure the peas inside. Shake the tambourine and tap it with your fingers for a lovely sound.

Songs and rhymes

Tip

Don't use rice as it is too small and will slip out between the staples.

Listen to the music

Accompany yourselves on instruments or clap your hands. Stop at 'music stops'; put your finger to your lips and say 'Sshhh!'

Listen to the music and play a tune,
Listen to the music and play a tune,
Listen to the music and play a tune,
Until the music stops.   SSSHHHHHHHH!

For the following verses sing and play as directed:

Listen to the music and play very slowly…

Listen to music and play very fast…

Listen to the music and play very softly…

Listen to the music and play very LOUDLY…

Painting activity

Put out paints, brushes and plenty of paper for 'free painting'.

Talk about

* Instruments: how many can the children name?

* Favourite sounds and favourite songs

* How instruments can be played in many different ways – plucked, banged, strummed, blown, shaken or struck; how they can be played alone or in a group such as a band or orchestra

We're marching to the drum

You only need one drum for this marching song. The leader bangs on the drum while leading, the others follow, playing instruments or not. Everyone must stop still and be as quiet as possible when the 'drum says STOP!' Each verse is played and sung as directed.

We're marching to the drum,
We're marching to the drum,
E-I-Aderry-O, we're marching to the drum,
And the drum says STOP!

We're running to the drum…

We'll tiptoe to the drum…

We're jumping to the drum…

Other verses can have stamping, skipping, hopping, and so on.

Stories

* *Baa Humbug! A Sheep with a Mind of His Own* by Mike Jolley and Susan Anne Reeves (Templar Publishing)

* *Katie Morag and the Grand Concert* by Mairi Hedderwick (Red Fox)

(Amy) can play the triangle

This song is sung to the tune of 'Have you seen the Muffin Man?' Encourage the children to choose an instrument and have a go at playing it while the group sings, naming the child and the instrument. Lots of praise and maybe a little applause after each verse will be welcome. Make sure only those children who are happy to perform are called on to do so.

(Amy) can play the triangle,
The triangle, the triangle,
(Amy) can play the triangle
And she can do it well.

(Daniel) can play upon the drum,
Upon the drum…

(Matthew) can play the rhythm sticks,
The rhythm sticks…

Barbara Melling

Other suggestions

*   Sing a song of sixpence

*   Oh we can play on the big bass drum

*   I am the music man

*   The grand old Duke of York

*   Rattlesnake Band
    Play instruments along to this one.

Finish with the Good-bye song on page 8.

Creative Activities for the Early Years

Craft activities

House collage

What you will need
* Large sheet (A2) of coloured paper
* Pictures of furniture and household contents (cut out beforehand from catalogues and magazines)

What to do
Have lots of pictures of everything you may find in a house, from beds and tables, to baths and televisions, curtains and saucepans, carpets, toys, lampshades and fireplaces.

Tip
Go through an old catalogue and cut out plenty of everything. Have lots of pictures of children's bedding, toys and food as these are always popular!

Place the paper on the table and cut the two top corners off to give a basic house shape. Draw a line across, between the cut-off corners, for the attic. Divide the rest of the paper into four rectangles to be the rooms.

Place the pictures in a large pile and allow the children to sort through, choose what they want, and glue onto the house.

Note
Let the children put things where they like, even if the arrangement is a bit unusual!

Tree house picture

What you will need
* Photocopiable tree house template (page 150)
* A4 brown paper
* Light coloured paper
* Green tissue paper

What to do
Before the session, cut a tree trunk shape from the brown paper (or colour it).

Tip
A rough shape is fine, but try and make sure it has a fat trunk, spreading out a little at the roots and at the top. There is no need for many branches.

Cut a door into the bottom of the trunk, leaving one side attached to allow it to open and close. Cut out one or two windows further up the trunk (these can be completely cut out). Turn the trunk over and tape or glue some light coloured paper to the back. Turn the trunk back again and add some details to the windows such as a window frame, a face looking out, a pot plant or a cat. Open the door and add something in the doorway such as a person or animal. Add a door knob and any further details you want. Finally glue pieces of scrunched-up green tissue paper to the top of the trunk for foliage and maybe some round the bottom for grass.

Try this idea!
Make a display of all the tree houses. Put them together on a wall to make a forest!

Thatched house

What you will need
* Cardboard box (such as a cereal box or shoe box)
* Thin card
* Straw
* Matchbox (or similar)

What to do
Cut a square of thin card that when folded will fit across the box as a roof. Paint the box with a mixture of paint and PVA glue and allow to dry. Glue or tape the 'roof' in place. Cut a 'V' shape into the matchbox and glue it to the top of the roof for a chimney. Paint the chimney. Using lots of glue, stick the straw to the roof. Add a door and windows and any other details to finish (shutters, ivy and so on).

Try this idea!
Paint a long piece of lining paper to look like a road. Set all the houses either side to make a lovely street!

Painting activity

Cut simple house shapes from paper, varying the sizes. Put them out with paints and brushes and allow the children to choose their own to paint.

Talk about

* Where the children live

* Type of home: house, flat, bungalow, caravan, castle

* Different rooms and their uses: cooking in the kitchen, sleeping in the bedroom, washing in the bathroom

Stories

* *Little Mouse Twitchy Whiskers* by Margaret Mayo and Penny Dann (Orchard Books)

* *Here's Buster – But Where's Teddy?* a lift-the-flap book by Rod Campbell (Campbell Books)

* *Big Bears Can!* by David Bedford and Gaby Hansen (Little Tiger Press)

Songs and rhymes

I know a house

I know a house, it's a cold old house,
A cold old house by the sea… Brrrrr!
  big shiver
If I were a mouse in that cold old house,
What a cold, cold mouse I would be… Brrrrr!
  big shiver and curl up small

Build a house with five bricks

Build a house with five bricks,
One, two, three, four, five.
  *use clenched fists for bricks, putting one on
  top of the other five times*
Put a roof on top
  *raise both arms above head with fingers
  touching*
And a chimney too
  straighten arms
Where the wind blows through…
WHOO WHOO.
  blow hard (or whistle)

Other suggestions

* There was a crooked man

* I went up one pair of stairs (see page 104)

* There was an old woman who lived in a shoe

* Wee Willie Winkie

* The work song
  From Disney's Cinderella.

* A spoonful of sugar
  From Disney's Mary Poppins. *Fun for dancing to with or without scarves.*

Finish with the Good-bye song on page 8.

Craft activities

Treasure chest

What you will need
* Photocopiable chest template (page 151)
* Thick paper
* Coloured shiny paper, silver and gold paper, cellophane

What to do
Cut a treasure chest shape from thick paper before the sesson begins. Add some details to the chest – a large lock, rivets or nails, wooden panels. Glue pieces of shiny paper, gold and silver paper and coloured cellophane onto the chest for the treasure, allowing it to pile up high and spill out over the sides.

Tip
Toffee and chocolate wrappers make perfect jewels!

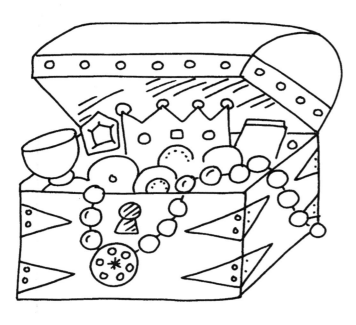

Pirate hat

What you will need
* Cardboard (flattened cereal box card)

What to do
Cut a pirate hat shape from the card (a fat sausage shape, approximately 25cm long, with a large lump along one edge rising to approximately 15cm). Paint this black using paint mixed with a little PVA, and allow to dry.

Either paint a simple skull and crossbones design directly onto the front of the hat, or cut one from a piece of white paper and glue it on.

Tip
The children may prefer to paint a large X with a blob in the middle, which will be perfect!

Cut another strip of card about 3cm wide and at least 30cm long, and attach it to the hat a little way in from one side. Place the hat against the front of the head and fit the strip of card around. Overlap the ends of the strip and stable or tape in place.

© Barbara Melling
www.brilliantpublications.co.uk

Pirate sword

What you will need
* Thick card
* Shiny paper, gold and silver paper

What to do
Before the session cut a sword shape from thick card. If using flattened cereal boxes, make the sword more of a dagger.

Using paint mixed with a little PVA glue, paint the sword and allow to dry.

Tip

To avoid too much wastage, cut out the blades and the hilts separately and tape them together.

Try this idea!
Tie a brightly coloured scarf round your waist and tuck in the pirate sword. Older children may enjoy having a scar or two drawn on with face paints.

Painting activity

Cut out some simple paper ships and allow the children to paint them. Encourage the children to paint their own flags. They don't all have to paint the Jolly Roger!

Talk about

* Pirates: keep it simple and do not make it too true to life! How they sailed the seas in big ships, buried treasure in chests on deserted islands, and even had parrots on their shoulders

* Has anyone been on a big ship on the sea?

* How many different types of treasure can the children think of: necklaces, rings, gold and silver coins, golden crowns, diamonds…

* You may want to have some chocolate coins to give out

Stories

* *Millie's BIG Surprise* by Gerald Rose (Anderson Press)

* *Captain Duck* by Jez Alborough (Picture Lions)

* *Tatty Ratty* by Helen Cooper (Corgi Childrens)

Songs and rhymes

A pirate went to sea, sea, sea

A 'pirate' version of this well-known clapping rhyme.

A pirate went to sea, sea, sea
To see what he could see, see, see
But all that he could see, see, see
Was the bottom of the deep blue sea, sea, sea.

I'm a little pirate

This action song is sung to the tune of 'I'm a little teapot.'

I'm a little pirate
In my hat.
> *point to hat*

I have a little sword
And I'm proud of that.
> *wave sword*

When I'm in my big ship
Sailing on the sea,
> *make wavy sea actions with hands*

I'm pleased I'm a pirate
> *stretch out hands*

And pleased I'm ME!
> *put both hands on chest*

Barbara Melling

Row, boys, row

This song can be sung sitting on the floor in pairs doing rowing actions or with an accompaniment of instruments

Row, boys, row,
As up the stream we go;
With a long pull
And a strong pull!
Row, boys, row.

Other suggestions

✳ The big ship sails on the alley alley-o (see page 70)

✳ Row, row, row the boat (see page 8)

✳ Bobby Shaftoe (see page 8)

✳ Bobbing up and down like this

✳ What shall we do with the drunken sailor?
A fast and furious song, brilliant for dancing a hornpipe to. It can be found on many recordings.

✳ I love to sail in my pirate ship
A variation of 'I love to rock in my big red boat' (see page 69) a lovely lullaby, perfect for calming down after playing at pirates.

Finish with the Good-bye song on page 8.

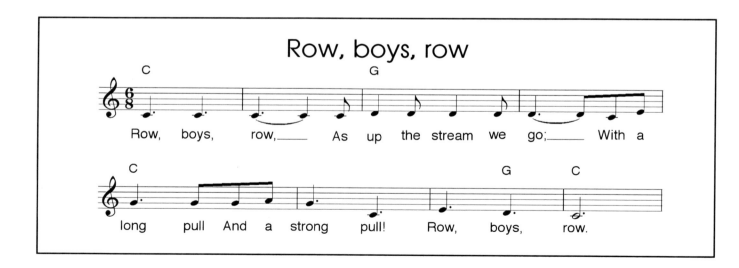

Creative Activities for the Early Years

Craft activities

Sand-castle

What you will need

* Large (A2) paper (orange or sandy colour optional)
* Sand (clean play sand can be bought from toy shops, or take a bucketful from your sandpit)
* Paper and tissue paper to decorate

What to do

Before the session cut out a sand-castle shape using as much paper as possible

Spread glue all over the paper and sprinkle on the sand. Cut out and decorate with paper shells and flags, and make seaweed from scrunched-up tissue paper. Stick them onto the castle.

Tip

Put newspaper down to catch the excess sand as this will make clearing up much easier!

Giant ice cream ◎ ○

What you will need

* A4 paper (light brown colour, or colour your own)
* Cotton wool
* Glitter (optional)

What to do

Before the session, cut out a cone shape from the paper (fold one of the shorter edges over to one of the longer edges, then cut across from about 21cm along the fold, in an arc).

Draw diamond shapes to decorate then bend the paper around into a cone and secure with tape. Scrunch up some waste paper (use the excess from cutting the cone!) and nearly fill the cone with it. Dab a little glue around the rim of the cone and pile in lots of cotton wool to make the ice cream.

Add details to the ice cream, maybe a chocolate flake (a roll of brown paper with darker lines drawn on), some hundreds and thousands (glitter), or perhaps some strawberry or chocolate syrup (coloured paint) dribbled over the top.

Photo frame ⊙⊙⊙

What you will need
* Thick card (cereal box card is fine)
* Sand
* Small shells (these can be collected from the beach or bought from shops) or pasta shells
* A holiday photo
* Ribbon

What to do
Before the session, cut two identical rectangles from thick card, approximately 16 x 12cm. Cut a smaller rectangle (about 12 x 8cm) from the centre of one of the pieces of card. (Cut from the middle and try not to cut the edge!)

Decorate the 'frame' with sand and shells stuck on with glue and leave it to dry completely. Place the 'backing' card the way of the photo, either landscape or portrait view. Carefully spread a 1cm thick line of glue around three edges of the backing, leaving the top side free from glue, and stick the decorated frame onto the backing. Allow to dry. Slide the photo in from the top (trim the photo if it sticks).

To display the photo frame on the wall, tape a loop of ribbon to the top back. To make a stand, cut a strip of thick card about 10 x 3cm, bend over about 2cm at one end and tape this end to the back of the frame.

Painting activity
Put out paper, brushes and paints and allow the children to 'free paint'.

Talk about
* Has anyone been to the seaside? What was it like?

* What can you find at the seaside – sand, pebbles, rocks, seaweed, starfish, crabs, sea gulls…

* If sand-castles were real, who could live in them? Perhaps kings and queens of the sea, or maybe mermaids or sea creatures!

Stories
* *Platypus* by Chris Riddell (Puffins Books)

* *Lucy and Tom at the Seaside* by Shirley Hughes (Puffin Books)

* *Bear in Sunshine* by Stella Blackstone (Barefoot Books)

Songs and rhymes

Seagull, seagull, sit on the shore

The actions to this song can be done standing or sitting: sit for the first verse; run about or shade eyes and point for the second, 'swim' around the room or in one place for the third.

Seagull, seagull, sit on the shore,
Sit on the shore, sit on the shore;
Seagull, seagull, sit on the shore,
Sail away my Santi Anna.

Puffin, puffin, follow the ship…
Sail away my Santi Anna.

Penguin, penguin, swim in the sea…
Sail away my Santi Anna.

What shall we do when we go out?

This fun action song goes to the tune of 'Have you seen the muffin man?' Form a circle, skip round for the chorus and stay in one place to do the actions.

Chorus

What shall we do when we go out,
We go out, we go out?
What shall we do when we go out,
When we go out to play?

Oh we can jump on the golden sand,
The golden sand, the golden sand.
Oh we can jump on the golden sand
When we go out to play.

Chorus

Oh we can swim in the deep blue sea…

Chorus

Oh we can SLURP on a big ice cream…

Other suggestions

* Row, row, row the boat (see page 8)

* Bobby Shaftoe (see page 8)

* If you're happy and you know it (see page 73)

* I love to rock in my big red boat (see page 69)

* Itsy bitsy teeny weeny yellow polka dot bikini

* The sun has got his hat on
  This jolly song is excellent for dancing to and can be found on lots of children's recordings.

Finish with the Good-bye song on page 8.

Seagull, seagull, sit on the shore

Sea - gull, sea - gull, sit on the shore, sit on the shore, sit on the shore; Sea - gull, sea - gull, sit on the shore, sail a - way my San - ti An - na.

Summer picnic

It is a good idea to do something different for the end of the summer term to mark the start of the holidays. A picnic is not only easy, it's lots of fun, especially if you plan it around a treasure hunt!

Idea!
Why not ask the children to each bring a teddy bear and have a teddy bears' picnic?

If your usual meeting place has an outside area you can use, then hold your picnic there. If not, why not use a local park or your garden, or even a group member's garden. If the weather is bad, just hold the picnic inside! Clear away the furniture to make lots of space on the hall floor. You could even decorate the room with branches and flowers.

Make sure you have some prizes, such as sweets, to reward the chidlren in the treasure hunt and picture searches.

Craft activity

Treasure baskets

To begin with have ready everything you need to make paper baskets (see page 72). As the children arrive they can get straight on and make their basket and not have time to get bored waiting for latecomers. If you are picnicking away from your hall, perhaps you can take along the baskets already made up, one for each child.

Treasure hunt

Give each child a list of things they have to find. An adult can help. Ask them to collect everything in their baskets. To help them work through their lists as much as possible by themselves, try to draw the items. The children will enjoy being able to understand what they are looking for.

Suggestions for the list

Outside
Three different leaves, a red/blue/yellow flower, a small stone, a fir cone, a feather, a daisy, a twig

Inside and outside
Cut-out coloured paper shapes: a red circle, a blue triangle, a yellow square, an orange crescent

    Creative Activities for the Early Years   © Barbara Melling
www.brilliantpublications.co.uk

Fun with pictures

Have a picture for each child (old greetings cards are excellent) and cut each one into four or five pieces. Keep back one piece of each picture, then mix all the other pieces together and place them round the room. Give out the pieces that were saved and encourage the children to look for the others to make up their picture.

Idea!

If you're having a teddy bears' picnic, you could have teddy bear pictures!

Cut out pictures of animals, food or toys from magazines (or use simple drawings) and hide them round the room. Ask questions such as 'What animal has a long nose?' 'Can you find an animal that roars?' The children must find the picture that answers the question.

Picnic food

Whether you all bring something towards a communal meal (see Christmas party, page 46) or each bring an individual picnic lunch, try to ensure that everyone sits down to eat at the same time. Spread rugs and blankets on the ground and keep close together. This is especially important if you are having your picnic in the park.

Stories, songs and rhymes

You may want to read a story or sing some songs. Let the children choose their favourites. If possible, bring some music outside along with a few instruments. Don't forget to include 'The teddy bears' picnic' (see page 17).

Finish with the Good-bye song on page 8, making special mention of any children not returning next term.

Fold

Cut

Creative Activities for the Early Years

© Barbara Melling
www.brilliantpublications.co.uk

Fold

Creative Activities for the Early Years

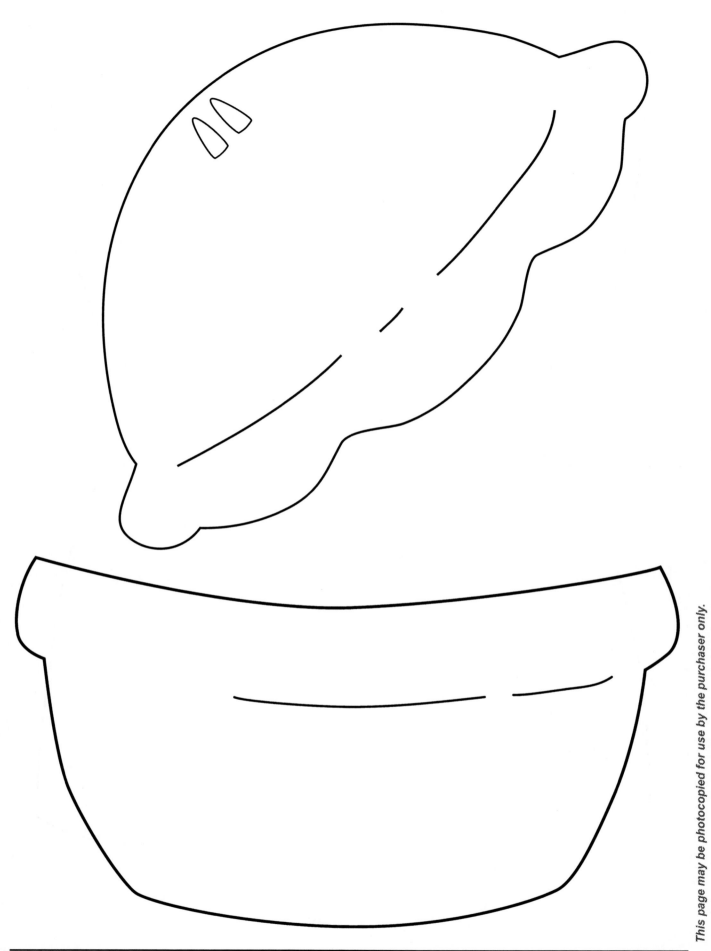

© Barbara Melling
www.brilliantpublications.co.uk

Creative Activities for the Early Years

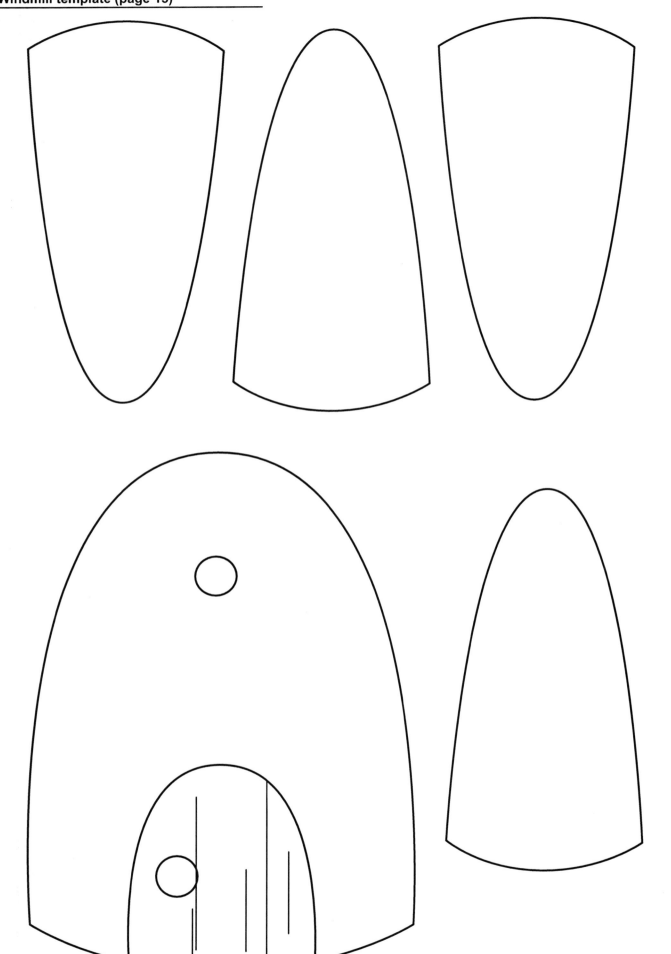

Creative Activities for the Early Years

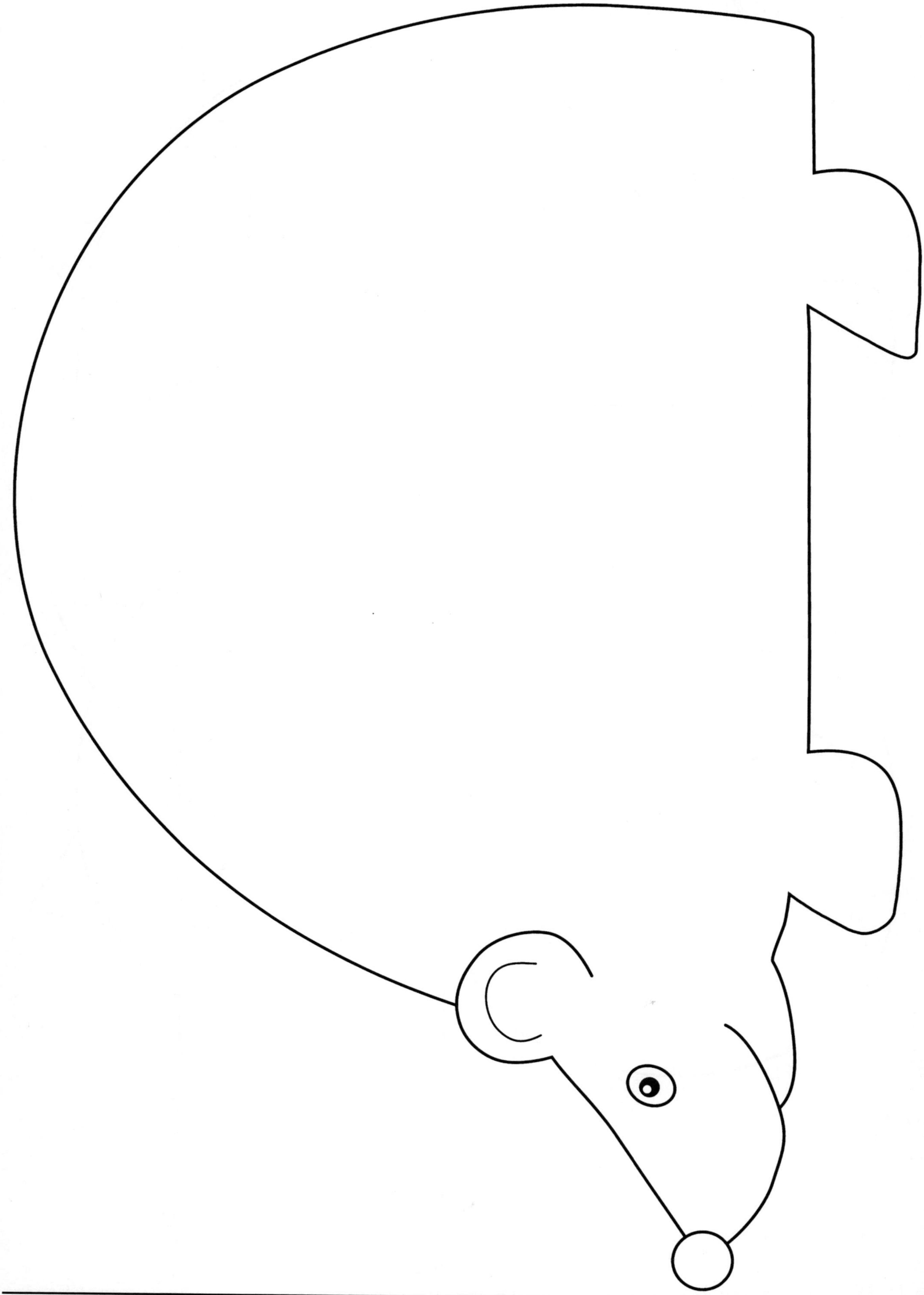

Creative Activities for the Early Years

Creative Activities for the Early Years

© Barbara Melling
www.brilliantpublications.co.uk

Fold

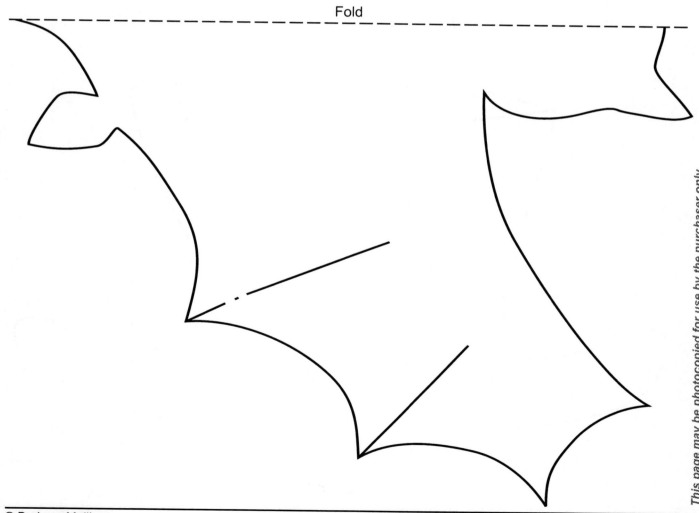

Creative Activities for the Early Years

Creative Activities for the Early Years

© Barbara Melling
www.brilliantpublications.co.uk

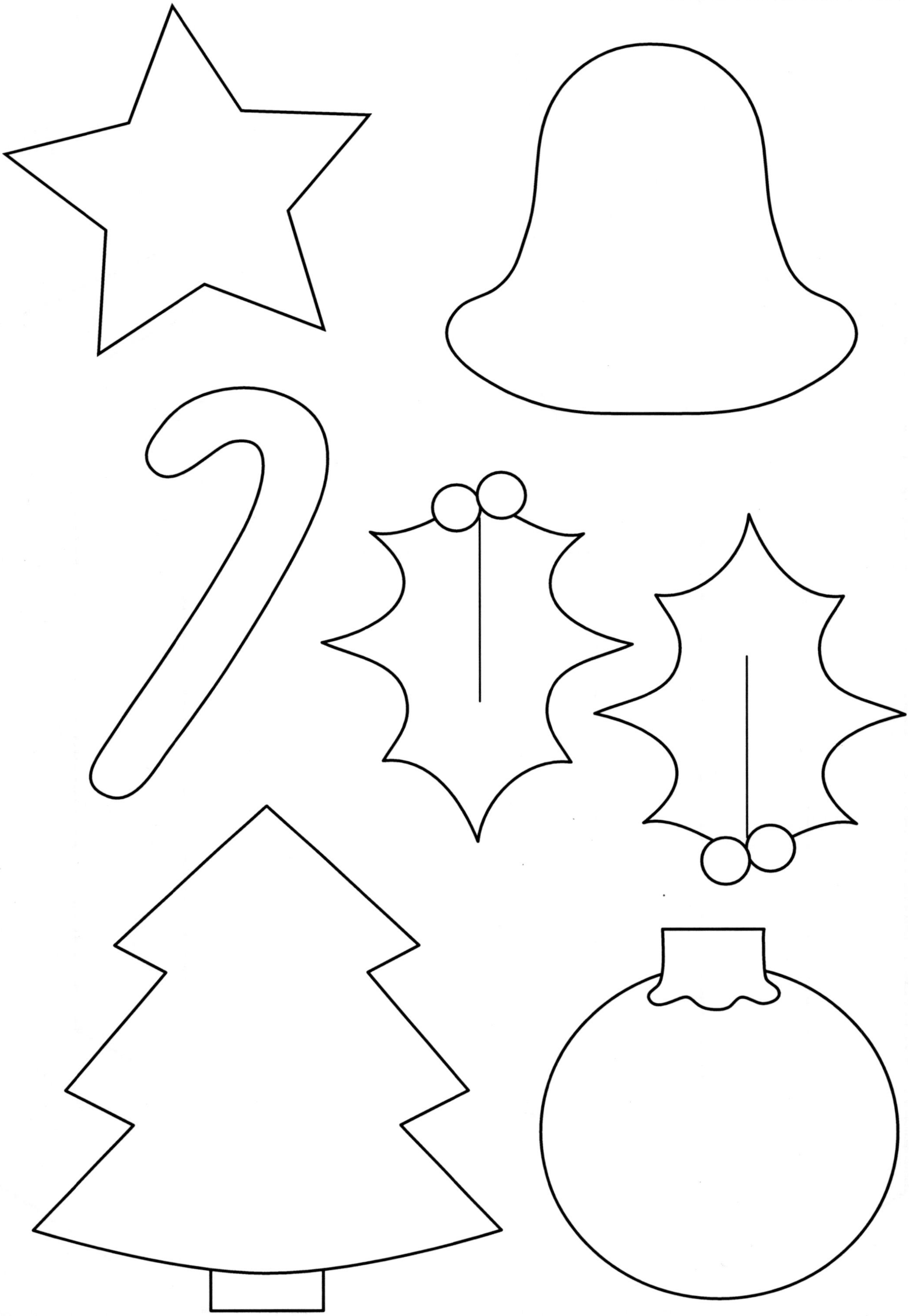

Creative Activities for the Early Years

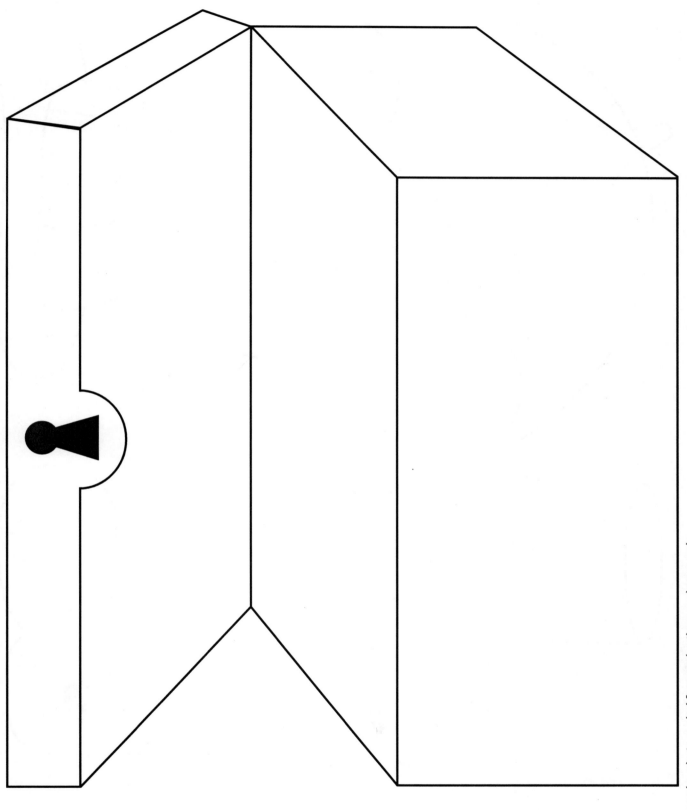

Creative Activities for the Early Years

© Barbara Melling
www.brilliantpublications.co.uk

Creative Activities for the Early Years

Creative Activities for the Early Years

Creative Activities for the Early Years

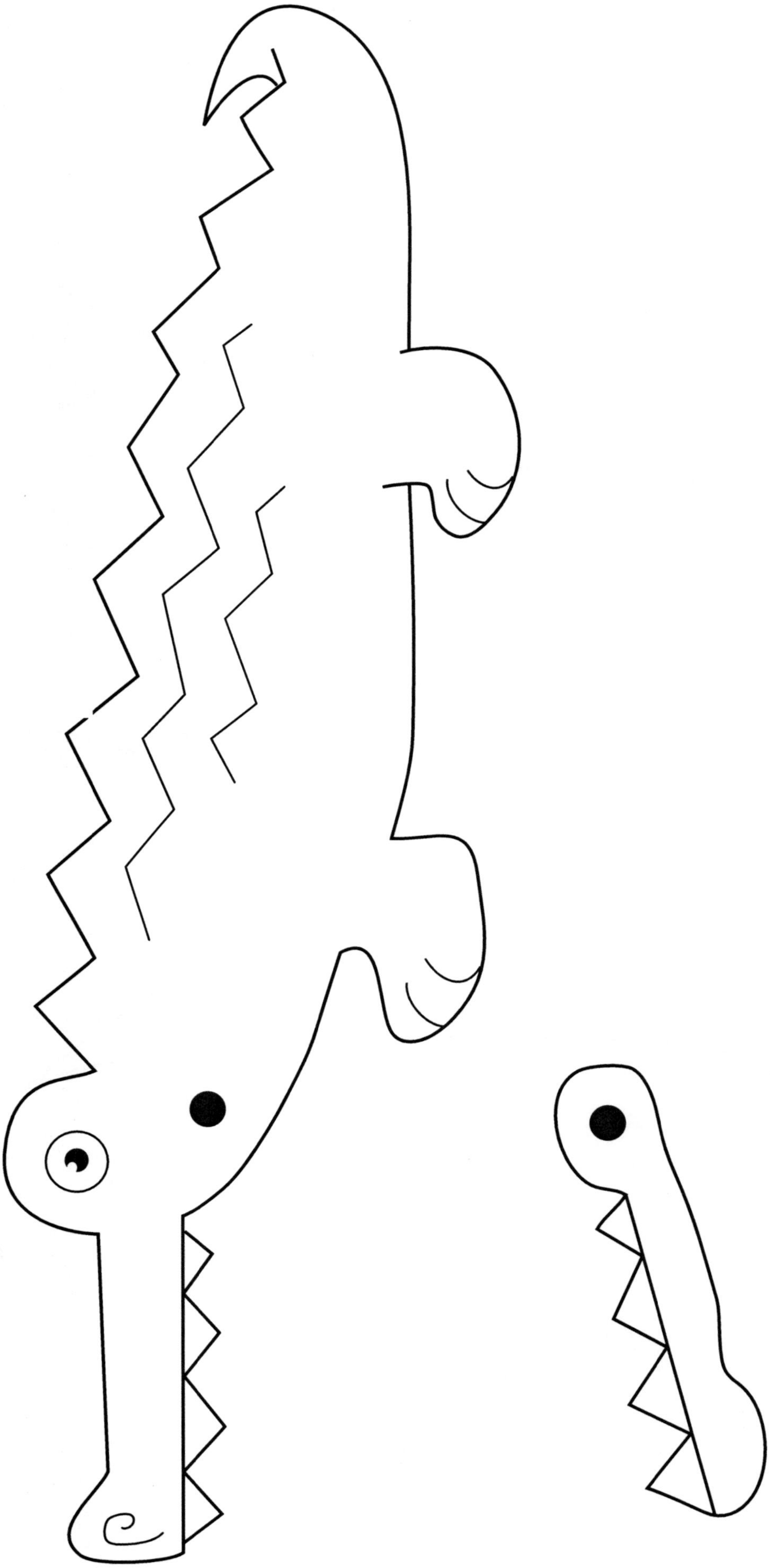

Fold

Creative Activities for the Early Years

Fold

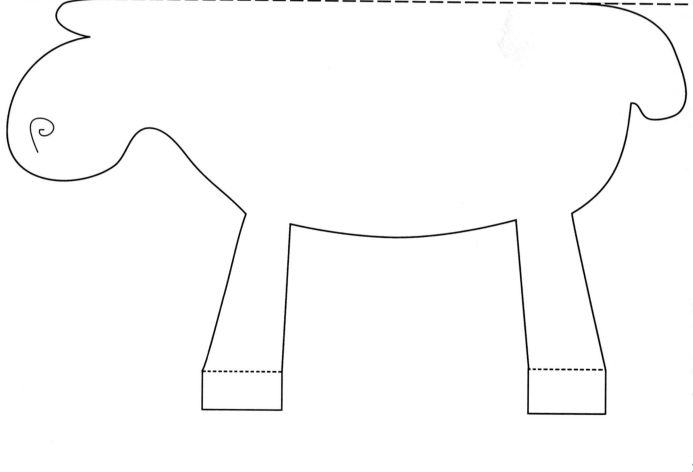

© Barbara Melling
www.brilliantpublications.co.uk

This page may be photocopied for use by the purchaser only.

Creative Activities for the Early Years

© Barbara Melling
www.brilliantpublications.co.uk

Creative Activities for the Early Years

Setting up a group

I wanted to start a group where the parents or carers of babies and young children could, and indeed were encouraged to, participate as there was none around at the time. I did so and found it remarkably easy and very popular! The adult and the child would work together, either on the same piece if the child was very young or needed help, or on separate pieces next to each other. This approach worked in two ways; first, the adult doing the same or similar activity reinforces the value of the child's work whilst also being on hand to help or make suggestions. Second, the adult enjoys it! It is as simple as that. Many parents said to me they loved having an excuse to play around with paint and glue, so much so that by request I had an adults only painting group, where they glued and cut and painted for an afternoon with no childeren in sight!

So if you have some spare time and want to do more with your young child give it a try, people will come from miles around to join you.

The room

First find a suitable room. This can be as simple or ambitious as you wish. Try to aim for a room to suit the size of the group you expect. I have found six to eight adults, not including myself, plus children is the right number for starting a group such as this. A larger group will need more organisation and there is more preparation to do beforehand.

You must have access to water and a sink of some kind, and of course at least one table and chairs, so remember these basic requirements when choosing. If you and a few friends are interested in holding a group it might be an idea to hold the sessions at someone's house and save the expenses of renting a room. As all the people will know each other there would be no worry about having strangers in your house, and everyone would help clear up!

Church halls are a good place to begin if you decide to hire a room. Most churches have a hall they let out for reasonable rents. Some have a smaller back room, which would be too small for larger groups such as nurseries but would be perfect for small groups. Alternatively, some shops have a room behind or above for hire. After a bit of searching you should be able to arrange a venue without too much difficulty.

Timing

The length of time required for a session will probably be between an hour and a half and two hours – any longer could be too much for very young children. When hiring a room remember to allow time for setting up and clearing away, up to an hour each end. If possible make a morning booking as most small children have a sleep after lunch and parents with older children will need to collect them from school. It is a good idea to follow the school term dates, not only because a lot of parents have older children at school and are unable to attend sessions in the holidays, but also because you will need a break.

Advertising

Advertising your group is essential. It only costs a few pence to put a handwritten poster in a post office window, while putting one up in a shop or library is free. Only bother with local newspapers if you intend to go into it in a big way and have a large group in a large hall. You can also ask to put a small pile of 'fliers' (small posters or notices) in your local sweetshop, chemist or on the post office counter, for example. Think of the places the parents of small children go regularly and target those.

The posters need not be elaborate: the simple ones often work best. Coloured paper has an immediate effect with handwritten information being just as good as printed, as long as it is neat and clear. Don't forget to put the day and time on the notice and also a phone number so people can book a place beforehand. That way you will have an idea of how many people are interested. It is up to you whether you include the cost of the sessions. Bear in mind that some places will not display a poster with a price on it (libraries, for example, usually have this policy).

Equipment

Paints

One of the main materials you will have to buy is paint. It is best to order this from a pre-school equipment catalogue, even if you have a very small group, because you will get a better price than in the shops and they can sell you small quantities. You can find out about catalogues by asking at your local playgroup for any old copies they may have and taking the telephone numbers. Shop around for the best deals. Stick to one type of paint: liquid paint is very good and less messy (a consideration for any group being held at home), but powder paints are very economical and are also worth considering.

Budget beater
You only really need five colours – red, blue, yellow, black and white. All other colours can be mixed from these. However it's worth buying a ready-mixed green as this is a very useful colour.

red + yellow = orange
blue + yellow = green
red + blue = purple
red + green = brown
red + white = pink

Add white or a touch of black to lighten or darken a colour.

Tip
Paint can be diluted by up to a third if you add washing-up liquid to it.

When using paint it is best to cover the table and the surrounding floor to prevent mess from spillage and also to make the clearing up easier. You can use newspapers, old plastic tablecloths or plastic sheeting (reasonably priced from DIY shops). Purpose-made attractive 'splash' sheets are available through the catalogues and are usually reasonably priced.

It is worthwhile investing in some non-spill plastic paint pots with opening and closing lids as they keep the paint fresh from one session to another, thereby reducing waste. You can also use one paintbrush per pot, allowing the colours to stay separate for longer. Yoghurt pots or even old saucers are quite adequate, but they need to be washed up each time!

Aprons

You will need aprons, both for the children and for yourselves as paint and glue can get everywhere. These can be bought through catalogues or shops, or you can easily make your own. Large old shirts or pyjama tops are perfect 'coveralls', if put on back to front. You might want to shorten the sleeves (one enterprising mother even used the off-cuts to make a matching floppy artist's hat!). If you are short of aprons, just suggest everyone wear old clothes.

Glue

You will need glue, and lots of it! White PVA glue is probably the best because it sticks just about anything, dries quickly, is non-toxic, and is easy to wash off clothes and hands. The best place to buy this is again through pre-school catalogues. Even with a very small group it is more economical to buy it in 5 litre bottles.

Budget beater
Glue can be diluted with a *little* water to make it go futher, but don't overdo it or it will lose its strength.

You will also need glue pots. Again, yoghurt pots or saucers are the answer. Remember to pour any unused glue back in the bottle as you can save more than you'd think by doing this.

Plastic spatulas are needed for spreading the glue. Much better than brushes and far easier to clean, they don't cost much and last for ever.

Scrap materials

Once you have your venue, starting date and group of people, you will need to start saving absolutely everything. Collect cardboard tubes, plastic bottles with lids of all shapes and sizes, cardboard cereal boxes and toothpaste boxes (in fact, any sort of box), yoghurt pots, ice cream pots. Save sweet wrappers, shiny foil, coloured cellophane, bubble plastic, paper plates, stones, shells, sticks, old newspapers, magazines, catalogues, egg boxes, wool, material, ribbons… in short, anything and everything you can think of!

Paper and card

Pre-school catalogues have a huge selection of paper and card and it is easy to get carried away. Remember that all the paper has to be stored somewhere and if you have more than you need this can present difficulties. Ideally you need some coloured paper, some black and some white. Mixed packs of A3 sheets are very good value and give you an assortment of colours. For extra value you can buy recycled packs. These come in white too and when cut in half are a perfect size for most children. A roll or two of plain white lining paper from your local DIY shop is a good idea for larger pictures and is also very good value. Thin card is the most useful; buy coloured and white. It comes in many sizes, from A3 and A4 sheets to pre-cut shapes. Finally, don't forget to keep all your cereal boxes. When flattened out these make a useful supply of *rough* cardboard.

Scissors

Children's scissors are essential. It is not necessary to have a pair each but try to have a reasonable number of pairs to avoid frustration. Be aware of the needs of left-handed people and try to have at least one pair of left-handed scissors. There is an excellent range of children's scissors available in pre-school catalogues and shops, including a good selection for children with various learning difficulties or special needs.

Children should be encouraged to use scissors to cut out as early as possible (under proper supervision of course). This greatly aids hand–eye co-ordination and helps enormously with letter formation and writing as they get older.

Sticky tape and paper straws

A few rolls of sticky tape are definitely needed, together with a box of art straws which can be bought from art shops or pre-school catalogues, are reasonably priced and last for ages!

Musical instruments

You can easily make some musical instruments to get you started.

Shakers
Pour some uncooked rice, dried peas, small stones or sand into plastic bottles with lids. Continue until the bottles are a third full. Experiment to find out what and how much to put in to make the best sound. Decorate the bottles with coloured ribbons and sticky paper.

Rhythm sticks (claves)
Buy a length of wooden dowelling (width 2–3cm) from your local DIY shop (or use an old, clean broom handle). Saw it into 15cm pieces and sandpaper the ends carefully to avoid splinters. Make sure you have an even number of sticks and use them in pairs to knock together. If you decide to paint or wood dye, them make sure the paint is non-toxic.

Bells
You will need some 15cm lengths of wooden dowelling (with the ends sanded) and some small individual bells, either bought cheaply from craft shops or salvaged from old toys. Attach three bells to a small hook then bend the hook over to secure the bells. Next screw the hook into the end of the dowelling. You then have a lovely instrument which can be used by even the youngest children.

Rasu-rasu
These are made from lengths of thick bamboo cane, easily obtained from garden shops. Cut to lengths of about 40cm. Cut small slits about 1cm apart not quite half way through the cane for about 20cms in the middle section. Sand off any splinters. Rub a 20cm pear stick or similar along the length of the cane to make a hollow rasping noise. If you wish, dye the cane and the stick using non-toxic wood dye. (These are not suitable for very young children.)

© Barbara Melling
www.brilliantpublications.co.uk

The instruments above should easily be enough to start with, but if you wish to buy any then triangles and tambourines are a good idea. They are reasonably priced and make a lovely sound. Drums are very popular but bring their own problems: if you only have a few there may be arguments, and if you have a lot you will all be deafened! Try to avoid flutes, pipes or any instrument that needs to be put in the mouth, because of the risk of spreading germs.

Keep all the instruments in a large box, or gathered in an old tablecloth which can be spread out on the floor to allow the children to help themselves.

Organising the sessions

Probably the best order for a session is to have the art and craft activities first. Aim to have at least three craft and one painting activity; the interest of both children and adults is kept fresh as they can 'graze' from one activity to another. Remember that the attention span of small children is quite short. It doesn't matter if they do not finish something – they can always come back to it if they want to.

Have an example of the art you are going to make that day on show so everyone can see how it has been made, but encourage people to have their own ideas. They do not have to slavishly follow the example. Allow the children to express themselves freely. Try to vary the painting activity with different techniques – for example sponging and printing as well as using brushes.

Drying paintings can sometimes be a problem as they can take up a lot of room if spread out to dry. One of the best ways is to have a 'washing line' complete with pegs. Put up a piece of strong string across a corner of the room and everyone can hang their paintings up to dry.

If you are in a hall it is a good idea to have a washing-up bowl of warm soapy water, perhaps placed on a chair at child height. Have a towel nearby. This arrangement allows them to wash their hands by themselves when they want to. It is not unknown for some children to wash their hands a lot, especially for the first two or three sessions. This may be the first opportunity the

child will have had to wash his or her hands without help from an adult.

I have suggested a few ideas you and the children can talk about during the art and craft time. It can be interesting and enjoyable to chat together about ideas connected with the theme of the day, and it can also encourage the adults to involve themselves totally in what is happening.

About an hour is probably long enough for the messy part of the session. After this it can be a good time for the children to sit down and have a drink and perhaps a snack away from the painting. You will thus be allowed to clear away most of the equipment whilst they are occupied.

For story time, move the tables and chairs to clear some floor space, or move to another room if you are at home. Everyone should be able to sit down and enjoy the story. Try to choose a short story with lots of pictures that is in some way connected to the theme of the session.

Tip ☆

Libraries are certainly the best place to go for books for story time. The librarians will be able to help you select suitable ones to try and may even lend you a term's supply of books at a time, to save you weekly trips!

Music and singing can occupy the final 30 minutes or so. Perhaps you could start with some simple nursery rhymes. These are wonderful for encouraging learning through repetition. It is very easy to make up actions to most nursery rhymes. Try to choose songs and rhymes connected with your theme if you can, although this is not always possible. You could then move on to songs involving clapping and body movement. Many songs, together with their movements are listed in this book, but there also are plenty of very good song books available in the shops and libraries. You will find the children develop their favourites, which have to be repeated again and again!

When it comes to the instruments, hand them out to the children or place them in the middle of the group, either in a box or on a blanket or tablecloth, for them to help themselves. Encourage everyone to have an instrument, including the adults. You can sing songs and accompany yourselves or march around the room to tunes such as 'The grand old Duke of York.' There are plenty of very good CDs and cassette tapes on the market with children's songs that are great to dance and march to. Most libraries have a good stock of tapes for children too. A CD or cassette player is all you need to accompany yourselves.

I have found it a good idea to have a collection of chiffon scarves ('floaties') which I have collected over time. These can be great fun: pile them in the middle of the floor and allow the children to choose one (or more, if possible), then play a tape of exciting dance music and encourage the children, and adults, to dance about, waving and twirling the scarves. This can introduce a different and important dimension into the music session; the scarves float around the dancers and help create an exciting 'finale'. Encourage the children to return their scarves to the bag at the end.

Once everything has been put away it is a good idea to sing a calming down song. Choose an old favourite like 'Ring-a-ring o' roses' or a lullaby if the children are very excited. End the session with the 'Good-bye song' where each child is named. This is helpful because the children feel they are valued as part of the group by being named in the song, and it helps the group to get to know each other if they do not already. You can make up a simple tune to go with it or borrow one from a well-known song.

Don't forget to mark the children's birthdays. You could sing 'Happy Birthday' after the 'floaties' and before the 'Good-bye song', when everyone is sitting down calmly. Perhaps give a balloon to the birthday child or a card.

Take home all work!

Encourage the children to take home as much of their work as they can and make sure the parents do too. Work should never be discarded or forgotten as the child will infer that his or her work is unimportant and of no value. Valuing their work and achievement is one of the most important gifts we as adults can give to our children and confidence built at this stage in their life will last for ever. Remember to praise everything, even the smallest scribble – although it might not seem like much to you it is an expression of the child's imagination and very precious. If one of the adults has made something alongside the children, this should also be valued.

Ready to go

To help you plan the running of your group, each session outlined in this book has a different theme and includes ideas for art and craft activities together with suggestions for stories and songs and rhymes that follow the theme through. The sessons can be mixed and matched to suit the needs of the group. I have found three Christmas sessions are needed, as there are many things for the children to make and some activities overlap from one week to the next.

It is fun to make the end of term a little special as it will usually be a few weeks before the group meets again and also some children may be moving on. The final session of the autumn term could be a party and a lovely way to finish the summer term is to have a picnic, either inside as usual or, if the weather permits, outside in a garden or park.

However you decide to run your pre-school creative groups, the main thing to remember is to have fun and for everyone to enjoy themselves!

Index of craft activities

Index of painting activities

© Barbara Melling
www.brilliantpublications.co.uk

Index of songs and rhymes

Page numbers in **bold** indicate where the song or rhyme appears in full.

Creative Activities for the Early Years

© Barbara Melling
www.brilliantpublications.co.uk